P9-CDM-081

76145

Combat Aircraft Library

British
Fighters
of World War II

Bill Gunston

Crescent Books
New York

Crescent Books

First English edition published by
The Hamlyn Publishing Group Limited 1982

All rights reserved.
This edition is published by Crescent Books,
distributed by Crown Publishers, Inc.
h g f e d c b a

Printed and bound in Italy

Created and produced by Stan Morse
Aerospace Publishing Ltd
10 Barley Mow Passage
London W4 4PH

© Copyright Aerospace Publishing Ltd 1982
Colour profiles and line diagrams © Copyright Pilot Press Ltd

All rights reserved. No part of this publication may be reproduced, stored in a retrieval system,
or transmitted in any form or by any means, electronic, mechanical, photocopying, recording
or otherwise, without the prior permission of the copyright holders.

All correspondence concerning the content of this volume should be addressed to Aerospace
Publishing Limited. Trade enquiries should be addressed to Crescent Books, New York.

ISBN: 0-517-374811

PICTURE ACKNOWLEDGEMENTS

The publishers would like to thank the following people and organisations for their help in
supplying photographs for this book.

Jacket front: Fox Photos. **Jacket back:** Imperial War Museum. **Page 1:** Charles Brown-RAF
Museum, Hendon. **4:** RAF Museum, Hendon. **10:** (bottom) RAF Museum, Hendon. **11:** (top)
RAF Museum, Hendon. **16:** RAF Museum, Hendon. **17:** (bottom) RAF Museum, Hendon.
18: (bottom) Imperial War Museum. **22:** Imperial War Museum/Imperial War Museum.
28: RAF Museum, Hendon/Imperial War Museum. **33:** Imperial War Museum. **38:** John Rawlings.
39: RAF Museum, Hendon. **40:** (bottom) RAF Museum, Hendon. **41:** (bottom) Imperial War
Museum. **46:** Imperial War Museum. **50:** RAF Museum, Hendon/RAF Museum, Hendon.
58: Imperial War Museum/RAF Museum, Hendon. **59:** RAF Museum, Hendon/RAF Museum,
Hendon. **61:** Charles Brown-RAF Museum, Hendon. **64:** (bottom) RAF Museum, Hendon.
67: RAF Museum, Hendon/Imperial War Museum, Hendon. **68:** (top) Imperial War Museum.
69: Imperial War Museum/RAF Museum, Hendon. **75:** Matthew Nathan. **76:** (bottom) Charles
Brown-RAF Museum, Hendon. **77:** Charles Brown-RAF Museum, Hendon/Charles Brown-RAF
Museum, Hendon. **78:** (bottom) RAF Museum, Hendon.

623.7464
GUN

1. Airplanes, Military
2. Royal Air Force
3. World War, 1939-1945 - Aerial operations
4. Aeronautics, Military
5. Fighters

623.7464
Gun
copy!

Foreword

The very fact that in the Battle of Britain the pilots of RAF Fighter Command unquestionably defeated the superior numbers of the previously invincible Luftwaffe shows that British fighters must have been pretty good. Yet in fact they were in many respects technically inferior to their opposite numbers, and available in far fewer quantities. By far the most important fighter, the Hurricane was obsolescent structurally, and for its assigned task and engine power it was larger than necessary. Both the Hurricane and the more modern Spitfire suffered from the weak firepower of rifle-calibre guns, and their use of a float-chamber carburettor made it impossible to follow German fighters in negative-g manoeuvres without the engine spluttering and cutting out.

Yet in the skilled hands of the RAF the Hurricanes and Spitfires inflicted the first military defeat Hitler's Third Reich had ever suffered, and made it possible for the Western democracies to build up their strength until on June 6, 1944 they were able to start the reconquest of Western Europe. By this time the Spitfire had changed so much it ought to have been given a new name. The Hurricane had at last been replaced by Typhoons and Tempests, though like their predecessor these were used mainly in the ground-attack role. From autumn 1940 the Bristol Beaufighter had served on all fronts and proved its ability to launch everything from bullets to torpedoes. Its partner, the wooden de Havilland Mosquito, matured as the best night interdiction aircraft of the war.

Thanks to Frank Whittle, Britain was the pioneer of the turbojet, and the world's first regular jet fighter squadron was not a Luftwaffe unit but No. 616 Sqn, Royal Air Force. Yet the Meteor was ordered in such small numbers and built with such lack of haste that the number delivered at the end of the war was just 1400 short of the Messerschmitt Me 262 total of 1430! The new German jets could do little to stem the tide of Allied advance but represented a new technology that had for years been in Britain's possession and should have been applied with far more vigour.

This volume tells the story of the trials and tribulations of Britain's struggle for air supremacy: a struggle as much with her own bureaucracy as with the enemy. Nonetheless it was a victorious struggle and one which contains many remarkable and fascinating aspects.

2/14/64; 3/2/64; 89.72 (10.82) American air force

Contents

Pre-War Fighters

Until the mid-1930s fighters were merely slightly more powerful versions of the fighting scouts of the Great War. Then engines, airframes, systems and armament changed dramatically.

When Germany invaded Poland at dawn on 1 September 1939 the latest Polish fighters were of a type designed in 1932 and flying in 1934. The United Kingdom's air capacity was in much the same situation, although the Royal Air Force did have a substantial number of modern Hurricanes in service, thanks almost solely to the patriotism and guts of the directors of Hawker Aircraft. They had the nerve to go into mass-production with the Hurricane long before the Air Ministry ordered it; and this was one of the things that saved the UK when it faced Germany in the autumn of 1940.

The Hurricane was by far the most important British fighter in the first year of war, mainly because of Hawker's early start and the establishment of a massive manufacturing and repair organisation to support it on a large scale. The fighter's origins went back to mid-1933 when Hawker's chief designer, Sydney Camm, roughed out the design for a new monoplane fighter derived from the Fury biplane then in production for the RAF. Powered by the 660-hp (492-kW) steam-cooled Rolls-Royce Goshawk engine then in favour, it had double the Fury's armament: four instead of two machine-guns.

The Fury II was the last of the Hawker biplane fighters, and though it looked much faster than the bluff two-bay-strutted Gauntlet the latter could outrun and outclimb it at high altitude. The Fury II's range of 260 miles was typical.

Had the Fury Monoplane been built the RAF would have been as outclassed as the Poles in 1939. Fortunately Camm decided to hold off, watching keenly as young Squadron Leader Ralph Sorley at the Air Ministry suggested fighters ought to have as many as eight guns, and Rolls-Royce switched effort from the Goshawk to a conventional liquid-cooled engine, similar to the Fury's Kestrel but of a larger capacity. By early 1934 Camm was designing a completely new and slightly larger monoplane fighter, powered by the PV.12 engine (later named the Merlin) of about 900 hp (671 kW). For almost the first time in a British fighter, it had retractable landing gear, the main gears folding inwards to be housed in the rather thick wing centre-section. By the time the prototype was being built provision was made for the unprecedented armament of eight machine-guns, in order to bring enough bullets on to the target in the expected brief shooting time available in future combat.

Unmistakably a Hurricane, the Hawker High-Speed Monoplane (K5083) built to specification F.36/34 was just sufficiently modern to sustain an important fighter production programme until September 1944. Yet compared with the Bf 109, which flew ahead of it, it lacked stressed-skin structure, aerodynamically profiled radiators, slats and a variable-pitch propeller, and was also much larger.

Hawker's new bird

The Hawker High-Speed Monoplane, serial number K5083, made its first flight at Brooklands (Weybridge) on 6 November 1935. It was larger than most existing fighters, with a span of 40 ft 0 in (12.19 m), and looked extremely modern. Structurally, however, it was somewhat dated, for instead of the new all-metal stressed-skin type of airframe, the High-Speed Monoplane was built by the traditional Hawker method of making a strong truss from metal tubes, with riveted and

Not many Hawker Fury II fighters remained on active service into World War II, though some saw combat with the South African Air Force in the Middle East. This example was camouflaged in 1937 whilst with No. 43 Sqn at Tangmere.

Pre-War Fighters

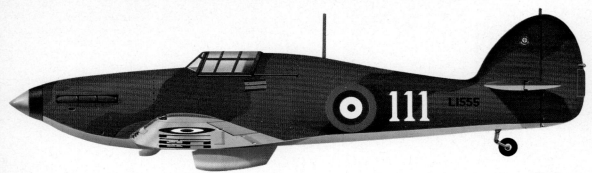

This Hurricane I, the ninth production aircraft, was issued to S/L J.W. Gillan, CO of No. 111 Sqn at Northolt, the first unit to receive the new fighter. In February 1938 Gillan flew L1555 by night from Turnhouse (Edinburgh) to Northolt at an average of 408 mph (657) with a strong tail-wind.

A Gloster-built Hurricane I, with Watts wooden propeller, in the odd 1939-40 marking in which the underside was half black (left) and half white (right).

Hawker Hurricane Mk IIC cutaway drawing key

1 Starboard navigation light
2 Starboard wingtip
3 Aluminium alloy aileron
4 Self-aligning ball-bearing aileron hinge
5 Aft wing spar
6 Aluminium alloy wing skinning
7 Forward wing spar
8 Starboard landing light
9 Rotol three-blade constant-speed propeller
10 Spinner
11 Propeller hub
12 Pitch-control mechanism
13 Spinner back plate
14 Cowling fairings
15 Coolant pipes
16 Rolls-Royce Merlin XX engine
17 Cowling panel fasteners
18 'Fishtail' exhaust pipes
19 Electric generator
20 Engine forward mounting feet
21 Engine upper bearer tube
22 Engine forward mount
23 Engine lower bearer tubes
24 Starboard mainwheel fairing
25 Starboard mainwheel
26 Low pressure tyre
27 Brake drum (pneumatic brakes)
28 Manual-type intertia starter
29 Hydraulic system
30 Bearer joint
31 Auxiliary intake
32 Carburettor air intake
33 Wing root fillet
34 Engine oil drain collector/breather
35 Fuel pump drain
36 Engine aft bearers
37 Magneto
38 Two-stage supercharger
39 Cowling panel attachments
40 Engine RPM indicator drive
41 External bead sight
42 Removable aluminium alloy cowling panels
43 Engine coolant header tank
44 Engine firewall (armour-plated backing)
45 Fuselage (reserve) fuel tank (28 Imp/127 litres)
46 Exhaust glare shield
47 Control column
48 Engine bearer attachment
49 Rudder pedals
50 Control linkage

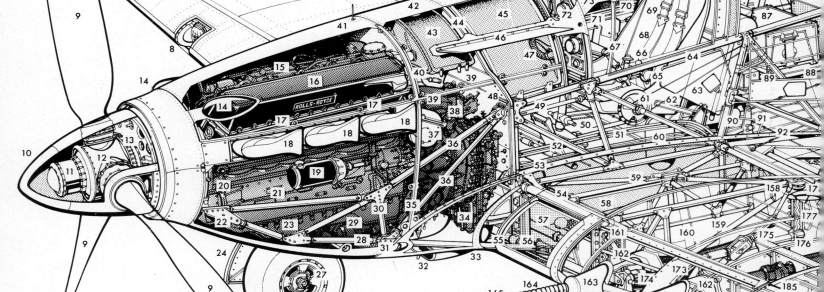

51 Centre-section fuel tank
52 Oil system piping
53 Pneumatic system air cylinder
54 Wing centre-section/front spar girder construction
55 Engine bearer support strut
56 Oil tank (port wing root leading-edge)
57 Dowty undercarriage ram
58 Port undercarriage well
59 Wing centre-section girder frame
60 Pilot's oxygen cylinder
61 Elevator trim tab control wheel
62 Radiator flap control lever
63 Entry footstep
64 Fuselage tubular framework
65 Landing lamp control lever
66 Oxygen supply cock
67 Throttle lever
68 Safety harness
69 Pilot's seat
70 Pilot's break-out exit panel
71 Map case
72 Instrument panel
73 Cockpit ventilation inlet
74 Reflector gunsight
75 Bullet-proof windscreen
76 Rear-view mirror
77 Rearward-sliding canopy
78 Canopy frames
79 Canopy handgrip
80 Plexiglas canopy panels

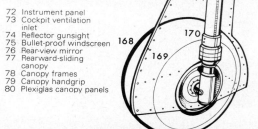

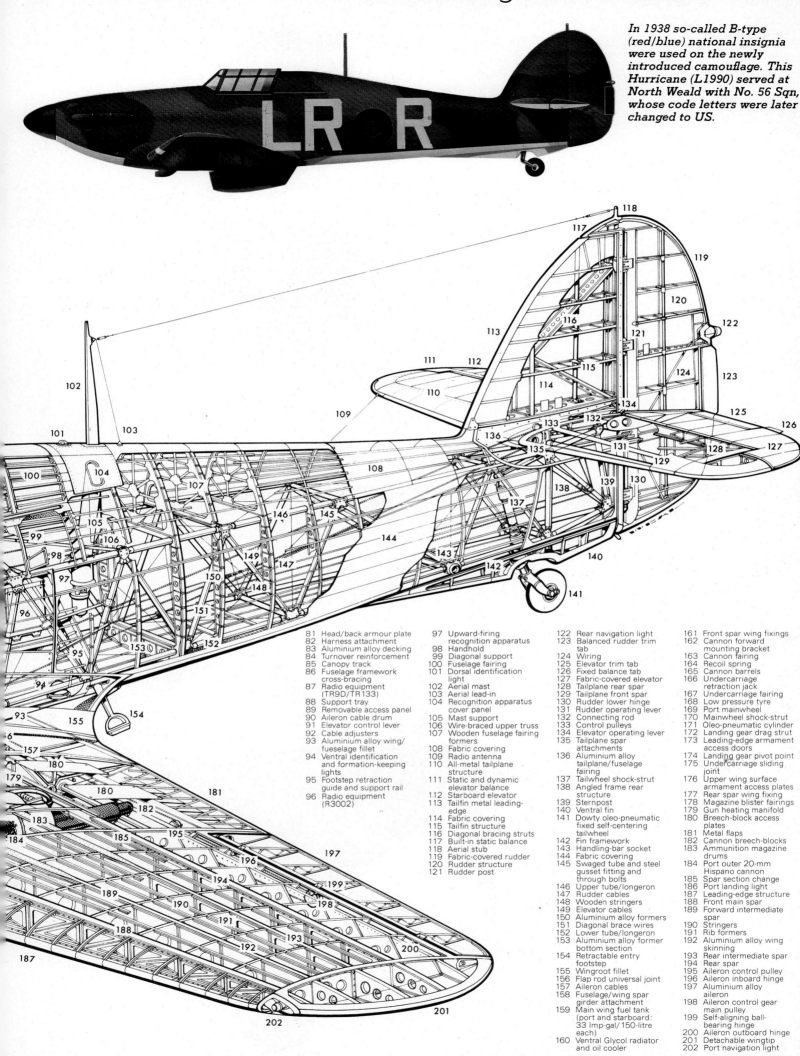

In 1938 so-called B-type (red/blue) national insignia were used on the newly introduced camouflage. This Hurricane (L1990) served at North Weald with No. 56 Sqn, whose code letters were later changed to US.

81 Head/back armour plate
82 Harness attachment
83 Aluminium alloy decking
84 Turnover reinforcement
85 Canopy track
86 Fuselage framework cross-bracing
87 Radio equipment (TR9D/TR133)
88 Support tray
89 Removable access panel
90 Aileron cable drum
91 Elevator control lever
92 Cable adjusters
93 Aluminium alloy wing/ fuselage fillet
94 Ventral identification and formation-keeping lights
95 Footstep retraction guide and support rail
96 Radio equipment (R3002)

97 Upward-firing recognition apparatus
98 Handhold
99 Diagonal support
100 Fuselage fairing
101 Dorsal identification light
102 Aerial mast
103 Aerial lead-in
104 Recognition apparatus cover panel
105 Mast support
106 Wire-braced upper truss
107 Wooden fuselage fairing formers
108 Fabric covering
109 Radio antenna
110 All-metal tailplane structure
111 Static and dynamic elevator balance
112 Starboard elevator
113 Tailfin metal leading-edge
114 Fabric covering
115 Tailfin structure
116 Diagonal bracing struts
117 Built-in static balance
118 Aerial stub
119 Fabric-covered rudder
120 Rudder structure
121 Rudder post

122 Rear navigation light
123 Balanced rudder trim tab
124 Wiring
125 Elevator trim tab
126 Fixed balance tab
127 Fabric-covered elevator
128 Tailplane rear spar
129 Tailplane front spar
130 Rudder lower hinge
131 Rudder operating lever
132 Connecting rod
133 Control pulleys
134 Elevator operating lever
135 Tailplane spar attachments
136 Aluminium alloy tailplane/fuselage fairing
137 Tailwheel shock-strut
138 Angled frame rear structure
139 Sternpost
140 Ventral fin
141 Dowty oleo-pneumatic fixed self-centering tailwheel
142 Fin framework
143 Handling-bar socket
144 Fabric covering
145 Swaged tube and steel gusset fitting and through bolts
146 Upper tube/longeron
147 Rudder cables
148 Wooden stringers
149 Elevator cables
150 Aluminium alloy formers
151 Diagonal brace wires
152 Lower tube/longeron
153 Aluminium alloy former bottom section
154 Retractable entry footstep
155 Wingroot fillet
156 Flap rod universal joint
157 Aileron cables
158 Fuselage/wing spar girder attachment
159 Main wing fuel tank (port and starboard: 33 Imp-gal/150-litre each)
160 Ventral Glycol radiator and oil cooler

161 Front spar wing fixings
162 Cannon forward mounting bracket
163 Cannon fairing
164 Recoil spring
165 Cannon barrels
166 Undercarriage retraction jack
167 Undercarriage fairing
168 Low pressure tyre
169 Port mainwheel
170 Mainwheel shock-strut
171 Oleo-pneumatic cylinder
172 Landing gear drag strut
173 Leading-edge armament access doors
174 Landing gear pivot point
175 Undercarriage sliding joint
176 Upper wing surface armament access plates
177 Rear spar wing fixing
178 Magazine blister fairings
179 Gun heating manifold
180 Breech-block access plates
181 Metal flaps
182 Cannon breech-blocks
183 Ammunition magazine drums
184 Port outer 20-mm Hispano cannon
185 Spar section change
186 Port landing light
187 Leading-edge structure
188 Front main spar
189 Forward intermediate spar
190 Stringers
191 Rib formers
192 Aluminium alloy wing skinning
193 Rear intermediate spar
194 Rear spar
195 Aileron control pulley
196 Aileron inboard hinge
197 Aluminium alloy aileron
198 Aileron control gear main pulley
199 Self-aligning ball-bearing hinge
200 Aileron outboard hinge
201 Detachable wingtip
202 Port navigation light

Hawker Hurricane

A Gloster-built Hurricane I of No. 501 Sqn in Battle of Britain colour scheme. To reduce drag a strip of fabric was attached over the muzzles of the guns with red dope, the bullets making neat holes as here.

Hawker Hurricane

SPECIFICATION

Type: single-seat fighter/fighter-bomber

Powerplant: (Mk IIB) one 1,280-hp (954-kW) Rolls-Royce Merlin XX V-12 piston engine

Performance: maximum speed 342 mph (550 km/h) at 22,000 ft (6705 m); maximum cruising speed 296 mph (476 km/h) at 20,000 ft (6095m); long-range cruising speed 212 mph (341 km/h); service ceiling 36,500 ft (11125 m); range with internal fuel 480 miles (772 km)

Weights: empty 5,500 lb (2495 kg); maximum take-off 7,300 lb (3311 kg)

Dimensions: span 40 ft 0 in (12.19 m); length 32 ft 2½ in (9.82 m); height 13 ft 1 in (3.99 m)

Armament: 12 0.303-in (7.7-mm) forward-firing machine-guns, plus two 250-lb (113-kg) or 500-lb (227-kg) bombs

Gloster-built Hurricane I of No. 85 Sqn, 1940. The squadron first used the hexagon badge on S.E.5a scouts in late 1917.

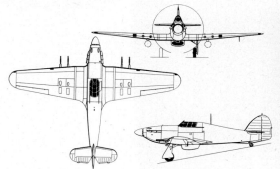

Hawker Hurricane IIC

Hawker Hurricane IIC, with 20-mm cannon.

bolted joints, covered with fabric. No modern variable-pitch propellers were available in the UK, so a traditional Watts propeller was fitted, with two blades carved from laminations of hardwood. And the chosen gun, the fast-firing belt-fed Colt-Browning, had been licensed to the UK only in July 1935, and few were available until 1937.

Hurricanes into service

After numerous modifications, the Hurricane Mk I reached No. 111 Sqn in December 1937, with an unbraced tailplane, extra small ventral keel under the tail, modified sliding cockpit canopy and ejector exhausts. Its armament comprised eight of the Browning guns, converted in the UK to fire 0.303 in (7.7 mm) rimmed ammunition and made under licence by the BSA Company. Boxes in the wings held 2,400 rounds, enough for about 20 seconds of continuous firing. Hawker brought in their sister-firm Gloster to help build Hurricanes, and also constructed a new factory at Langley, near Slough, so that 497 had been delivered by the time World War II began. In 1939 a few Hurricanes flew with licence-built American Hamilton-type propellers, and also with the

The first Hurricane squadron, No. 111 Sqn, showing all nine aircraft. In 1938 this seemed the last word in modern defence; and indeed Britain would almost certainly have been defeated in 1940 without the Hurricane.

The first great book to come out of the air war in 1940 was **Fighter Pilot** *by Paul Richey. He served in France with No. 85 Sqn, here seen climbing to meet the enemy after their Hurricane Is had been fitted with variable-pitch Rotol propellers.*

British Rotol, but panic conversion from the fixed-pitch two-bladed unit did not happen until well into 1940. In April 1939 Hawker made a modern wing, with normal spars, ribs aligned fore/aft, and stressed-skin covering, and this later became standard along with a bullet-proof windscreen, pilot seat armour and self-sealing tanks.

Gloster could not begin making Hurricanes immediately because the company had only delivered its first Gladiator in February 1937 and had to continue building this biplane until April 1940. Though designed to a 1930 Air Ministry specification, the Gladiator was much delayed and by 1937 was becoming obsolete. A fabric-covered metal-framed fighter, it did at least have four guns; originally these comprised two Vickers guns in the fuselage and two Lewis guns under the lower wings, but later the new Brownings were fitted in all four locations. Like other biplanes the Gladiator was supremely agile, and very agreeable to fly, but in performance and firepower it

Gloster Gladiator

SPECIFICATION
Type: single-seat biplane fighter
Powerplant: (Mk II) one 830-hp (619-kW) Bristol Mercury IX radial piston engine
Performance: maximum speed 257 mph (414 km/h) at 14,600 ft (4450 m); service ceiling 33,500 ft (10210 m); range 440 miles (709 km)
Weights: empty 3,444 lb (1562 kg); maximum take-off 4,864 lb (2206 kg)
Dimensions: span 32 ft 3 in (9.83 m); length 27 ft 5 in (8.36 m); height 11 ft 7 in (3.53 m); wing area 323 sq ft (30.01 m²)
Armament: four forward-firing 0.303-in (7.7-mm) machine-guns

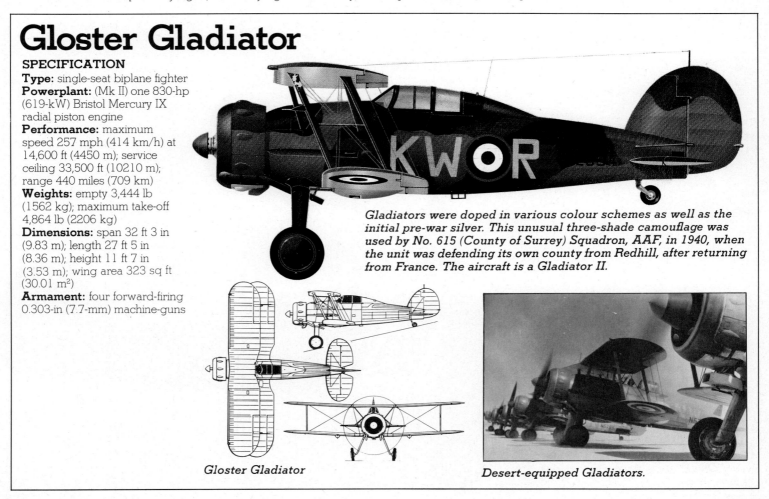

Gladiators were doped in various colour schemes as well as the initial pre-war silver. This unusual three-shade camouflage was used by No. 615 (County of Surrey) Squadron, AAF, in 1940, when the unit was defending its own county from Redhill, after returning from France. The aircraft is a Gladiator II.

Gloster Gladiator

Desert-equipped Gladiators.

Before receiving Hurricanes No. 87 Sqn had flown Gladiators, this profile showing the peacetime squadron marking on the CO's aircraft. Home base was Debden, but when the (Hurricane) unit returned from France it re-formed at Exeter.

The Gladiator was one of the most successful British military aircraft in winning foreign sales. One of the early customers was Belgium, whose Aéronautique Militaire received 22 in late 1937. All saw action, like the machines exported to Norway and Finland also. Unit was 2e Regt La Comète at Diest-Schaffen.

When the Luftwaffe appeared over Norway on 9 April 1940 there were just seven serviceable Gladiators in the Jageravdeling (fighter flight) at Oslo-Fornebu. They had lately been converted back to wheels from the winter ski gear shown here.

In early 1940 the Finnish Ilmavoimat (air force) received 30 Gladiators from RAF stocks, but their poor performance, firepower and protective attributes resulted in them proving a great disappointment. The skis were locally produced.

Another overseas operator of the Gladiator was Portugal, whose Arma de Aeronáutica received 30 (but really wanted Spitfires).

Supermarine Spitfire I/II

SPECIFICATION

Type: single-seat day fighter
Powerplant: one 1,030-hp (768-kW) Rolls-Royce Merlin II or III V-12 piston engine
Performance: maximum speed 355 mph (571 km/h) at 19,000 ft (5790 m); service ceiling 34,000 ft (10360 m); range 495 miles (797 km)
Weights: empty 4,796 lb (2175 kg); maximum take-off 5,332 lb (2419 kg)
Dimensions: span 36 ft 10 in (11.23 m); length 29 ft 11 in (9.12 m); height 11 ft 5 in (3.48 m); wing area 242.0 sq ft (22.48 m²)
Armament: eight 0.303-in (7.7-mm) Browning machine-guns

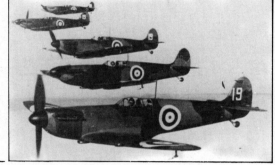

The eighth production Spitfire I was assigned to S/L Henry Cozens, CO of No. 19 Sqn at Duxford, the first to receive this new fighter in October 1938.

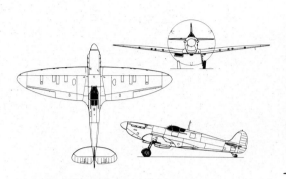

Supermarine Spitfire Mk IIA

Spitfire Mk Is of No. 19 Sqn, RAF.

was far below Germany's Messerschmitt Bf 109E. Gladiators fought valiantly over France and Norway (and were used by the Finns and several other nations) but spent most of the war in the Mediterranean theatre.

Best of all the pre-war designs was the Supermarine Spitfire, destined to be the only Allied fighter in production throughout the war. Designed by Reginald Mitchell, who had previously designed flying-boats and racing seaplanes of totally different construction, the Spitfire was, like the Hurricane, the result of enterprise by its designer. Again like the Hurricane, an official specification was later written around it. Though it used the same engine as the Hurricane, the Spitfire was smaller, and it had a modern stressed-skin airframe. The wing was most unusual, because it had curved leading and trailing edges leading to pointed tips, which were distinctive but did little for performance and were difficult to make. Structurally the wing was equally odd, because the strength lay in the thick leading-edge skin and single spar, forming a small box of D-section; and the spar was assembled from stacks of channel sections nesting one inside another. The engine radiator, which in the Hurricane was under the belly, was in the Spitfire placed

These Spitfires are probably scrambling from Biggin Hill with No. 92 Sqn during the Battle of Britain. At this time there was no uniformity on whether, on the right side, the squadron code should be ahead of the roundel or behind it.

This pre-war picture is believed to show No. 19 or No. 66 Sqn Spitfire Is peeling off behind a Blenheim in early 1939. Before the outbreak of war the number of Spitfires available was insignificant.

well back under the right wing, with the oil cooler in a smaller duct under the left wing. The main landing gear legs were like those of the Bf 109, hinged near the root of the wing and retracting outwards.

Best all-round fighter in the world

The prototype (K5054) of what was originally called the Supermarine Type 300, was flown at Eastleigh (today Southampton Airport) on 5 March 1936. It handled superbly, and despite the narrow track and relatively huge engine was found to be simple to taxi on the ground. On take-off the torque tended to swing the nose to the left and had to be countered by a 'bootful of right rudder'. In the air the 'Spit' was superb, and after provision of self-sealing tanks, armour and the missing four guns (absent from early examples) to make up the full octet, was the best all-round fighter in the world when it reached No. 19 Sqn at Duxford in June 1938. By that time the pathetic output of the parent firm, which only managed to complete five aircraft by the time of Munich in September 1938, was being rapidly accelerated, and plans were in hand to build Spitfires at a much faster rate at a giant Shadow Factory built by the Nuffield organisation at Castle Bromwich, east of Birmingham. Mitchell died of tuberculosis in June 1937 and was succeeded by equally brilliant and dedicated Joe Smith who was to develop the Spitfire out of all recognition.

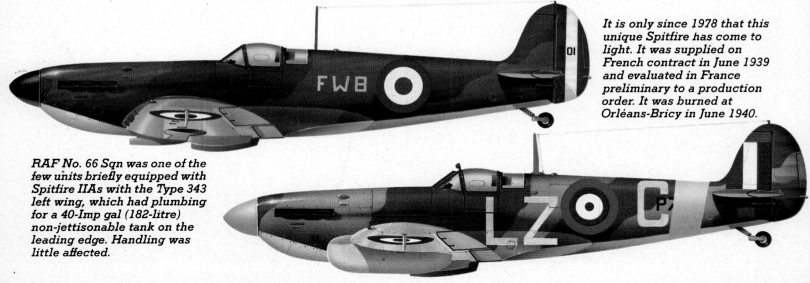

It is only since 1978 that this unique Spitfire has come to light. It was supplied on French contract in June 1939 and evaluated in France preliminary to a production order. It was burned at Orléans-Bricy in June 1940.

RAF No. 66 Sqn was one of the few units briefly equipped with Spitfire IIAs with the Type 343 left wing, which had plumbing for a 40-Imp gal (182-litre) non-jettisonable tank on the leading edge. Handling was little affected.

Early Wartime Fighters

For all practical purposes the RAF relied totally upon the Hurricane and the rather better but scarcer Spitfire in the crucial first year of the war. In armament and combat tactics it had to make up for years of neglect.

During the Battle of Britain No. 303 (Polish) Sqn, RAF, had flown Hurricanes. It re-equipped in 1941 with the Spitfire VB, having begun the process of conversion with the Mk IIA in late 1940. This was the CO's Mk VB.

The UK's need for fighters in 1940 was desperate. Had this been foreseen some of the pre-war prototypes might have gone into production, an outstanding example being the Martin-Baker M.B.2 which was almost exactly as fast as a Spitfire despite having fixed landing gear! This machine had numerous engineering features officially described as 'far in advance of existing practice', but its flight stability needed perfecting and in 1938 the need for such serviceable machines was not so pressing. Another fighter of the 1937-8 period, the Gloster F.5/34, was startlingly similar in almost all respects to the Japanese Zero, but it, too, was rejected.

One fighter which was accepted for production, but turned out to be a disappointment, was the Westland Whirlwind. This was the most radical of seven proposals to meet Air Ministry specification F.37/35 for a fighter carrying the very heavy armament of four 20-mm cannon. Though only fractionally larger than the Hurricane, it had twin engines, the chosen Rolls-Royce Peregrine of 885 hp (660 kW) being a development of the familiar Kestrel. It had coolant radiators inside the wing centre section, offering minimal drag (later designers found such radiators could actually provide propulsive thrust); the guns were grouped in the short nose; and the tailplane was mounted very high on the tall fin to keep it clear of the wake from the powerful Fowler-type flaps.

Early Wartime Fighters

Despite these flaps the Whirlwind had what was then considered a very high landing speed, making it difficult to operate from short grass fields. Wing loading (weight supported by unit area of wing) was high, being almost twice that of a Hurricane Mk I, which made manoeuvrability poor. Worst of all, the Peregrine was very unreliable, and only two squadrons operated with Whirlwinds, flying almost all of their missions in the role of attack bombers. With Merlins, operating from the 6,000 ft (1830 m) runways that by 1942 were common, the Whirlwind might have been a most formidable fighter, but such a machine was never built.

Another disappointment was the Boulton Paul Defiant. This was the successful design to meet a 1935 specification for a two-seat fighter armed with a four-gun turret. The Defiant was a pleasant aircraft to fly, rather like a Hurricane but with modern stressed-skin construction, but the concept of putting the guns in a turret proved mistaken. Inevitably, with the same engine as a Hurricane but greater weight and a slightly smaller wing, the Defiant was poor in manoeuvrability as well as in flight performance and firepower, and was soon relegated to such duties as air/sea rescue and target towing. Some became quite successful night-fighters, but it was surely a waste of resources to go on making Defiants into 1943, to a total well in excess of 1,000.

When the idea of a turret-armed fighter was still exciting, a far more ambitious specification was written, F.11/37, for a fighter with a turret armed with four 20-mm cannon. Unlike those of the Defiant, these guns were to be able to fire straight ahead, aimed by the pilot in the usual way, as well as trained by the gunner right round 360°. The winning design was again by Boulton Paul, the P.92 being a very fast and powerful machine with two Rolls-Royce Vulture or Napier Sabre engines of each some 2,000 hp (1492 kW). The P.92 was cancelled before it flew, in 1940, but a low-powered scale model, the P.92/2, was flown to test the basic idea.

In fact the RAF had rather overlooked the need for a long-range escort fighter, and the gap was expected to be filled by an attractive single-seat twin-engined fighter by Gloster, the G.39 to

P7110 was one of the last batch of Whirlwinds, delivered in December 1941. In many ways an outstanding aircraft, it was crippled by low-power engines with poor reliability. A high landing speed was also held against it, but in fact it landed slower than the Fw 190 which was used from every kind of rough front-line strip.

N1535, the first of a batch of 202 Defiant Is, was the aircraft of the CO of No. 264 Sqn, the first unit to become operational with this turret-armed two-seater. In flight it extended two retractable radio masts from its underside.

Westland Whirlwind

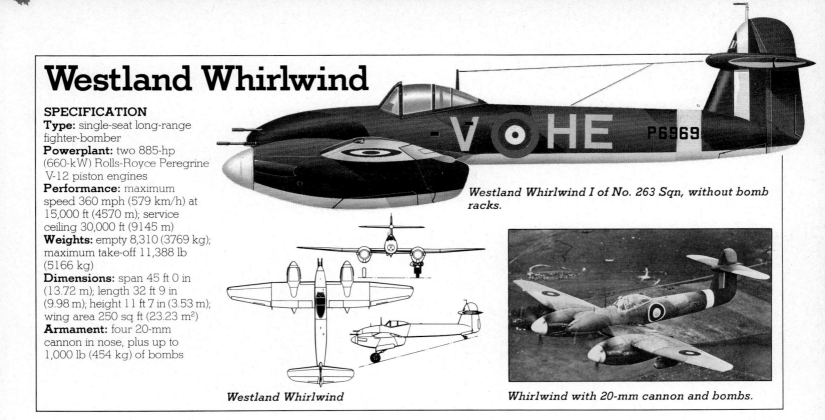

SPECIFICATION

Type: single-seat long-range fighter-bomber

Powerplant: two 885-hp (660-kW) Rolls-Royce Peregrine V-12 piston engines

Performance: maximum speed 360 mph (579 km/h) at 15,000 ft (4570 m); service ceiling 30,000 ft (9145 m)

Weights: empty 8,310 (3769 kg); maximum take-off 11,388 lb (5166 kg)

Dimensions: span 45 ft 0 in (13.72 m); length 32 ft 9 in (9.98 m); height 11 ft 7 in (3.53 m); wing area 250 sq ft (23.23 m²)

Armament: four 20-mm cannon in nose, plus up to 1,000 lb (454 kg) of bombs

Westland Whirlwind I of No. 263 Sqn, without bomb racks.

Westland Whirlwind

Whirlwind with 20-mm cannon and bombs.

This Whirlwind I, one of a production total of 114, was retained by Westland Aircraft and registered as G-AGOI in late 1945. The rest saw action, chiefly as target of opportunity bombers over northern Europe in 1941-2.

specification F.9/37. Though this handled well and almost as fast as a Spitfire (despite its large fuel capacity and armament of two cannon and four machine-guns), it was abandoned. The only long-range fighters at the start of the war were about 200 Bristol Blenheim light bombers which had hastily been fitted with a belly installation of four machine-guns. These became the first radar-equipped night-fighters.

In 1940-1 the tough and easily repaired Hurricane continued to be the most important RAF fighter, developed in several improved versions with metal-skinned wings and the more powerful Merlin XX driving the excellent Rotol RX.5/2 constant-speed propeller. The improved wings could carry heavier armament: by 1941 the RAF thus had the choice of eight machine-guns (Hurricane Mk IIA), 12 machine-guns (Mk IIB) or four 20-mm cannon (Mk IIC). Further options included drop tanks (extra fuel tanks, jettisoned when empty) or two bombs, initially of the 250 lb

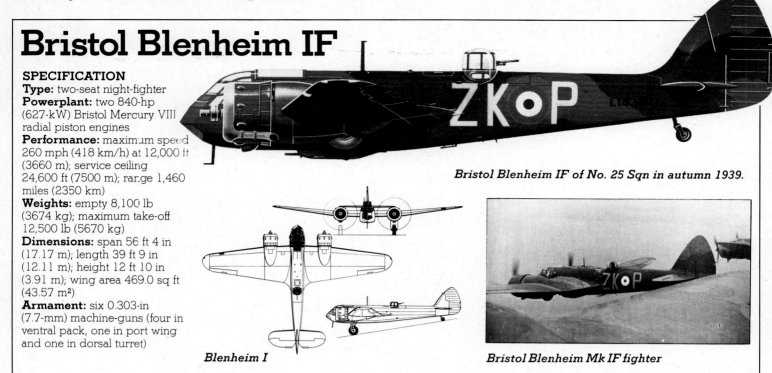

Bristol Blenheim IF

SPECIFICATION
Type: two-seat night-fighter
Powerplant: two 840-hp
(627-kW) Bristol Mercury VIII
radial piston engines
Performance: maximum speed
260 mph (418 km/h) at 12,000 ft
(3660 m); service ceiling
24,600 ft (7500 m); range 1,460
miles (2350 km)
Weights: empty 8,100 lb
(3674 kg); maximum take-off
12,500 lb (5670 kg)
Dimensions: span 56 ft 4 in
(17.17 m); length 39 ft 9 in
(12.11 m); height 12 ft 10 in
(3.91 m); wing area 469.0 sq ft
(43.57 m²)
Armament: six 0.303-in
(7.7-mm) machine-guns (four in
ventral pack, one in port wing
and one in dorsal turret)

Bristol Blenheim IF of No. 25 Sqn in autumn 1939.

Blenheim I

Bristol Blenheim Mk IF fighter

(113 kg) size but later of double this weight. In 1942 the Hurricane Mk IID began a career of tank-busting with two 40-mm high velocity cannon, and a year later Hurricanes went into action with eight 60-lb (27-kg) rockets, a weapon pioneered in the Soviet Union in 1934-5. From 1940 Hurricanes were also made by Cancar (Canadian Car and Foundry) at Fort William, Ontario, and the final species in 1943 was the versatile Mk IV with a 1,620-hp (1209-kW) Merlin driving a four-blade propeller, and with a Universal Wing able to carry any of the wide range of guns or underwing loads. Total production of Hurricanes was 14,231.

Biplane Hurricane

One odd Hurricane version not built in quantity was the Slip-Wing or Bi-Mono Hurricane, built by Hillson in Manchester in 1940. Range was increased by the carriage of extra fuel in a new upper wing, slightly larger than the original, which effectively turned the Hurricane into a biplane. When the top-wing tanks were empty the pilot jettisoned this wing complete with its struts, leaving a normal Hurricane to do battle. As described later, many Hurricanes fought at sea, but plans for a seaplane version were not realised. Seaplane fighters were suddenly thought of in April 1940 to fight in Norway, and from 1941 four Spitfires were actually flown as seaplanes. They were extremely good seaplanes, but the RAF dropped the idea and never had a fighter seaplane in World War II.

The first Blenheim IF fighter squadron was No. 25, but it was soon followed by the AAF No. 604 'County of Middlesex' Squadron at Northolt, whose aircraft are seen here in summer 1939. They were soon afterwards pioneering with Mk II AI radar.

According to the test pilots the Gloster F.9/37 was an outstanding aircraft, and many observers thought that it should have gone into production. This photograph shows a Taurus radial-engined example of this long-range single-seater, the other prototype having the Peregrine V-12.

The Hurricane IID tank-buster was the chief carrier of the 40-mm Vickers S-type gun, hung under the wings so that each shot depressed the nose of the aircraft noticeably. This Mk IID served with the most famous 'can openers' unit, RAF No. 6 Sqn.

Trials on Salisbury Plain with a Hurricane IID mounting two 40-mm guns.

Bristol Blenheim IF

Bristol Blenheim Mk IF shown in the pre-war livery of No. 25 Sqn, Royal Air Force (the first unit to equip with the type) at Hawkinge, Kent.

Early Wartime Fighters

The Hillson FH.40 bi-mono experiment. Originally a Hawker-built Hurricane I (L1884) shipped to Canada, the aircraft was returned to Britain where it underwent trials with a jettisonable upper wing, intended to provide extra lift to enable the aircraft to be flown out of small airfields; the scheme was abandoned in 1943.

The Spitfire itself, however, developed in an ever-increasing number of versions. After the very similar Mks I and II that fought in the Battle of Britain, the next mass-produced version was the Mk V with a strengthened fuselage to take the more powerful 1,470-hp (1097-kW) Merlin 45 and related engines, driving better constant-speed propellers. No fewer than 6,479 Spitfires Mk Vs were made, in three major sub-types: the Mk VA with the original eight machine-guns, the Mk VB with two 20-mm cannon and four machine-guns, and the Mk VC with four cannon. Like the Hurricane, the Spitfire learned to carry bombs and drop tanks, though at first these loads were on the centreline instead of under the wings. Joe Smith's engineers also developed something Camm never did for the Hurricane: a range of different wings with the normal span of 36 ft 10 in (11.23 m), a clipped wing of 32 ft 2 in (9.80 m) and a long pointed wing of 40 ft 2 in (12.24 m) span. The clipped wing gave more rapid roll and in most respects improved performance at low

An echelon of tropicalised Hurricane IIB fighter-bombers over the Tunisian front around December 1942. Some Hurricanes were hard-pressed to reach 300 mph (483 kmh) but even with the tropical filter the IIB was able to reach 330 mph (531 kmh), which took care of most things over Tunisia apart from the Bf 109.

Soon after the German invasion of the Soviet Union on 22 June 1941 the RAF sent No. 151 Wing to help fight the Luftwaffe. This Hurricane IIB of No. 81 Sqn was based at Vaenga in September 1941, with Soviet number code in place of the individual aircraft letter. Later some were fitted with skis and even converted as two-seaters. They were given to the Russians when the RAF units were recalled in December 1941.

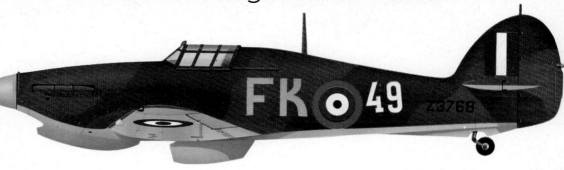

One of the more isolated Hurricane units was RAF No. 30 Sqn based at Ceylon (mainly at Negombo for local defence) in late 1942, at a time when even that island did not appear safe from invasion. BG827 was a Gloster-built Hurricane IIB.

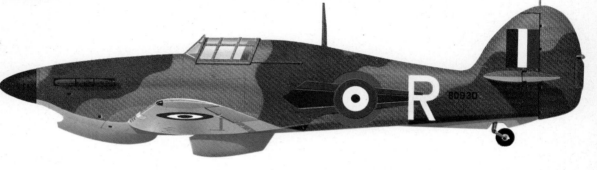

One of the RAF squadrons that sought to retain its pre-war insignia on the fuselage was No. 73, which on this Langley-built Hurricane IIB overlapped the yellow ring on the fuselage roundel. Code letters (TP) were in consequence omitted.

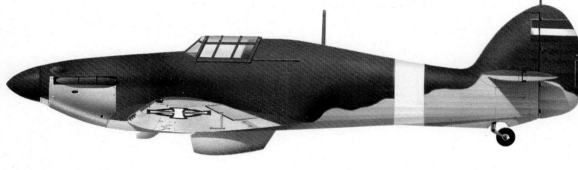

When Yugoslavia was invaded by the Germans in April 1941 its chief fighters included the Hawker Fury and Hurricane. This aircraft was one of a batch of Hurricane Is made under licence at Zemun. Several escaped to Paramythia in Greece only to be destroyed there by bombing.

In September 1941 the Air Ministry began to introduce modified colour schemes for British military aircraft, notable features of which were replacement of dark earth (brown) by sea grey in the upper-surface camouflage and, from June 1942, a narrowing of the yellow and white rings (to one eighth of total radius) in the roundel and of the white band in the fin flash. The new scheme, which also included a yellow stripe along the leading edge, is seen here on Hurricane IIC HL603 of No. 1 Sqn.

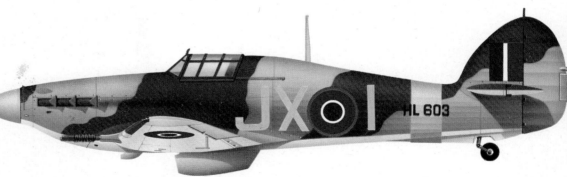

Believed to be the sole Hurricane in Australia during World War II, V7476 (the hyphen was added 'down under') was one of the first Mk I aircraft to have stressed-skin wings. It served the RAAF on communications.

Supermarine Spitfire V

This Spitfire VA, built at Supermarine's Southampton (Woolston) plant, was one of the last armed with machine-guns only. It was the personal aircraft of Douglas Bader when he was leader of the Tangmere Wing in early 1941. Later he collided with a Bf 109 over France and became a noted prisoner of war, and escaper.

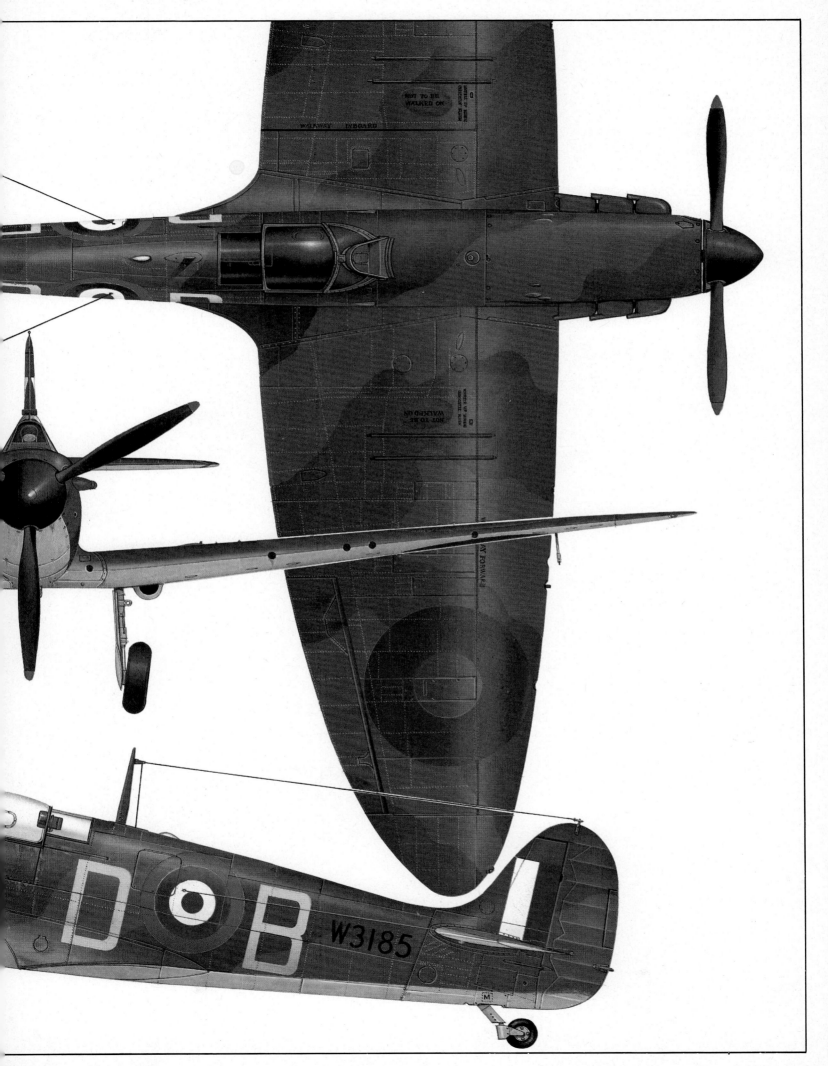

Early Wartime Fighters

Supermarine Spitfire VB cutaway drawing key

1 Aerial stub attachment	16 Elevator control lever	28 Fuselage angled frame	43 Cockpit aft glazing
2 Rudder upper hinge	17 Tailplane spar/fuselage	29 Battery compartment	44 Voltage regulator
3 Fabric-covered rudder	attachment	30 Lower longeron	45 Canopy track
4 Rudder tab	18 Fin rear spar (fuselage	31 Elevator control cables	46 Structural bulkhead
5 Sternpost	frame extension)	32 Fuselage construction	47 Headrest
6 Rudder tab hinge	19 Fin front spar (fuselage	33 Radio compartment	48 Plexiglas canopy
7 Rear navigation light	frame extension)	34 Radio support tray	49 Rear-view mirror
8 Starboard elevator tab	20 Port elevator tab hinge	35 Flare chute	50 Entry flap (port)
9 Starboard elevator	21 Port elevator	36 Oxygen bottle	51 Air bottles (alternative
structure	22 IFF aerial	37 Auxiliary long-range fuel	rear fuselage stowage)
10 Elevator balance	23 Port tailplane	tank	52 Sutton harness
11 Tailplane front spar	24 Rudder control lever	(29 gal/132 litre)	53 Pilot's seat (moulded
12 IFF aerial	25 Cross shaft	39 Dorsal formation light	Bakelite)
13 Castoring non-retractable	26 Tailwheel oleo access	40 Aerial lead-in	54 Datum longeron
tailwheel	plate	41 HF aerial	55 Seat support frame
14 Tailwheel strut	27 Tailwheel oleo shock-	42 Aerial mast	56 Wingroot fillet
15 Fuselage double frame	absorber		57 Seat adjustment lever

58 Rudder pedal frame	70 Fuselage lower fuel tank
59 Elevator control	(37 gal/168 litre)
connecting tube	71 Firewall/bulkhead
60 Control column spade	72 Engine bearer attachment
grip	73 Steel tube bearers
61 Trim wheel	74 Magneto
62 Reflector gunsight	75 "Fishtail" exhaust
63 External windscreen	manifold
armour	76 Gun heating "intensifier"
64 Instrument panel	77 Hydraulic tank
65 Main fuselage fuel tank	78 Fuel filler cap
(48 gal/218 litre)	79 Air compressor intake
66 Fuel tank/longeron	80 Air compressor
attachment fittings	81 Rolls-Royce Merlin 45
67 Rudder pedals	engine
68 Rudder bar	82 Coolant piping
69 King post	83 Port cannon wing fairing

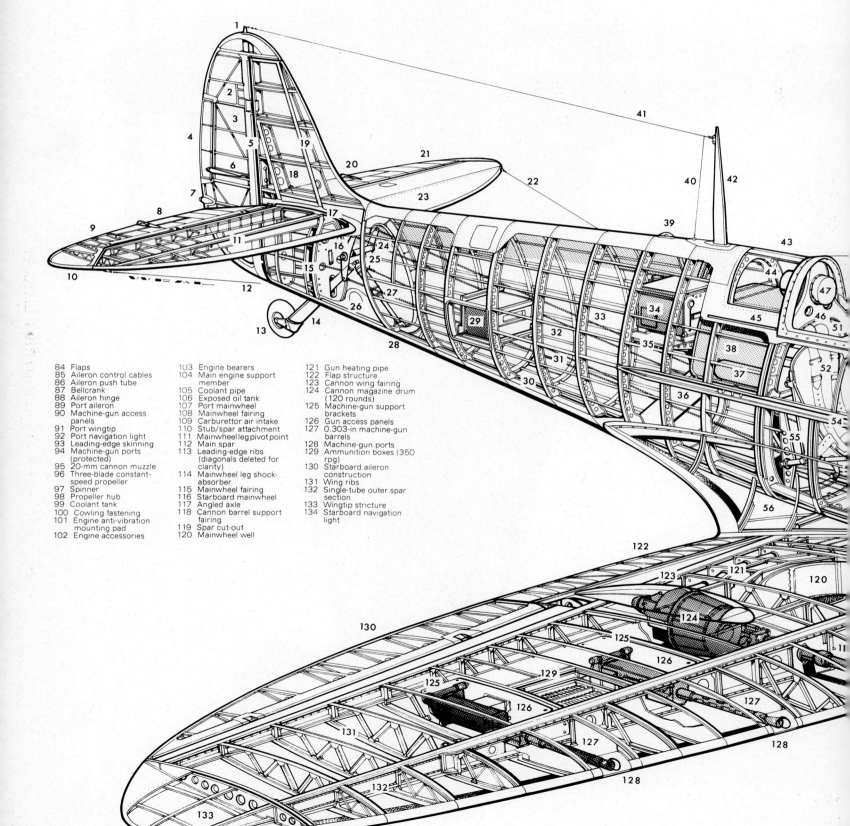

84 Flaps	103 Engine bearers	121 Gun heating pipe
85 Aileron control cables	104 Main engine support	122 Flap structure
86 Aileron push tube	member	123 Cannon wing fairing
87 Bellcrank	105 Coolant pipe	124 Cannon magazine drum
88 Aileron hinge	106 Exposed oil tank	(120 rounds)
89 Port aileron	107 Port mainwheel	125 Machine-gun support
90 Machine-gun access	108 Mainwheel fairing	brackets
panels	109 Carburettor air intake	126 Gun access panels
91 Port wingtip	110 Stub/spar attachment	127 0.303-in machine-gun
92 Port navigation light	111 Mainwheel leg pivot point	barrels
93 Leading-edge skinning	112 Main spar	128 Machine-gun ports
94 Machine-gun ports	113 Leading-edge ribs	129 Ammunition boxes (350
(protected)	(diagonals deleted for	rpg)
95 20-mm cannon muzzle	clarity)	130 Starboard aileron
96 Three-blade constant-	114 Mainwheel leg shock-	construction
speed propeller	absorber	131 Wing ribs
97 Spinner	115 Mainwheel fairing	132 Single-tube outer spar
98 Propeller hub	116 Starboard mainwheel	section
99 Coolant tank	117 Angled axle	133 Wingtip stricture
100 Cowling fastening	118 Cannon barrel support	134 Starboard navigation
101 Engine anti-vibration	fairing	light
mounting pad	119 Spar cut-out	
102 Engine accessories	120 Mainwheel well	

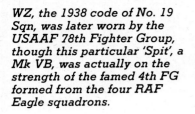

WZ, the 1938 code of No. 19 Sqn, was later worn by the USAAF 78th Fighter Group, though this particular 'Spit', a Mk VB, was actually on the strength of the famed 4th FG formed from the four RAF Eagle squadrons.

Spitfire IIA (presentation aircraft paid for by donations from the Observer Corps, later the Royal Observer Corps) flown by the CO of No. 41 Sqn at Hornchurch, S/L Don Finlay (pre-war Olympic hurdler).

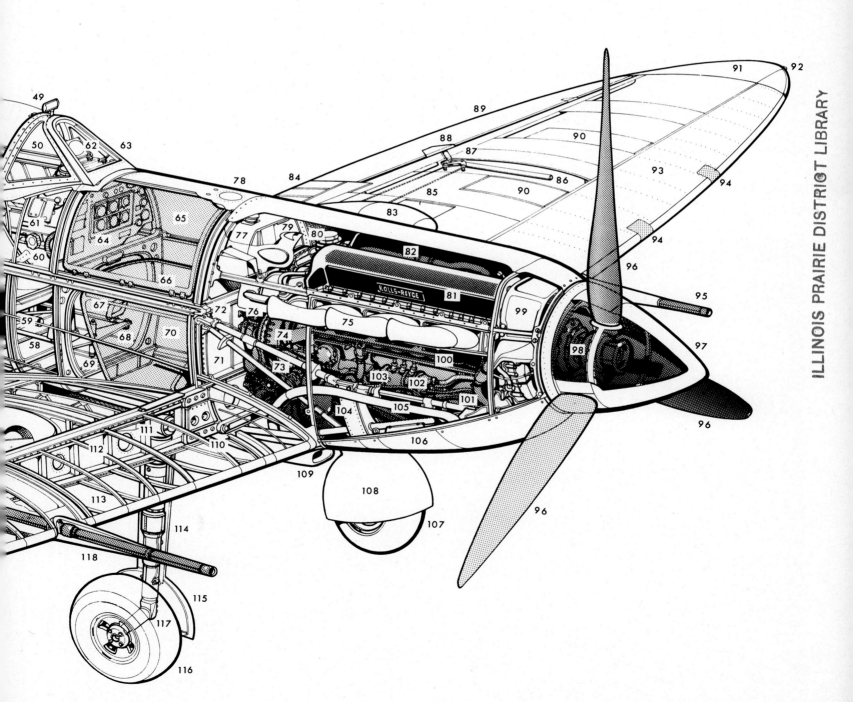

ILLINOIS PRAIRIE DISTRICT LIBRARY

Early Wartime Fighters

In many ways the wooden Miles M.20 was a remarkably fine fighter, and it is a pity it ran up against totally negative thinking on the part of the Air Staff. This example, the M.20/4, was built to Naval specification N.1/41, later becoming DR616.

altitudes, and in 1941-2 the clipped Mk VB was the best the RAF could offer to match the Focke-Wulf Fw 190. The long pointed wing was for ultra-high altitudes, as explained in Chapter 4.

In the summer of 1940 the need for fighters was so urgent that there were even plans for fitting guns in lightplanes, and in the tiny Percival Mew Gull racer, proposed in a fractionally enlarged form with retractable landing gear. One company, Miles Aircraft, even designed and built a fighter from scratch and flew it in much less than three months. This M.20 was an outstanding machine, the first fighter to have the teardrop type of canopy giving all-round view (and soon universal on almost all fighters) and despite fixed landing gear having a speed near that of a Spitfire and much higher than a Hurricane. It was highly manoeuvrable, and in range and ammunition capacity was superior to all other British single-seat fighters, but the crisis passed and the M.20 never went into production.

Tropicalised Spitfire VC fighter-bombers of No. 417 (RCAF) Sqn, on the dusty Italian front in 1943. At this time, early 1943, No. 417 was converting to the high-flying Mks VII and VIII.

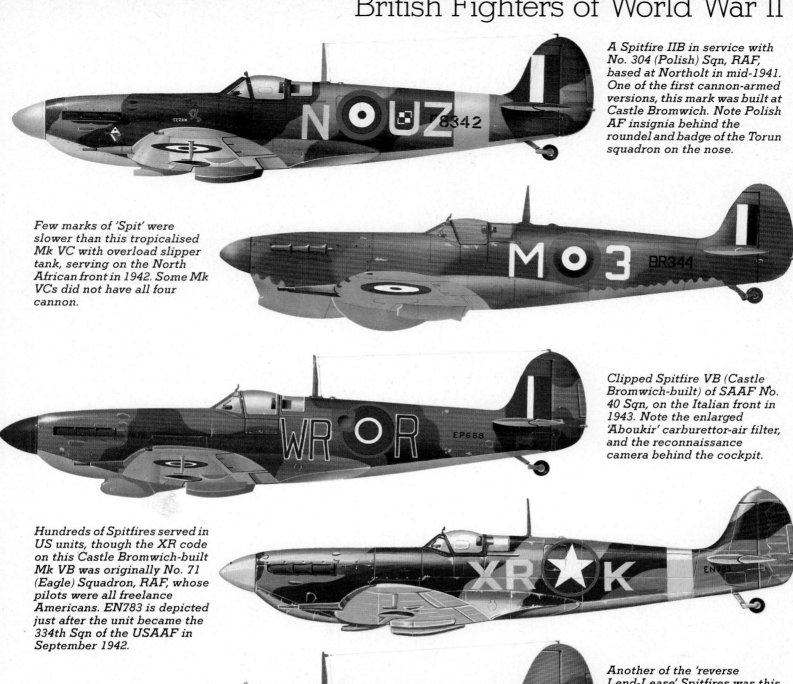

A Spitfire IIB in service with No. 304 (Polish) Sqn, RAF, based at Northolt in mid-1941. One of the first cannon-armed versions, this mark was built at Castle Bromwich. Note Polish AF insignia behind the roundel and badge of the Torun squadron on the nose.

Few marks of 'Spit' were slower than this tropicalised Mk VC with overload slipper tank, serving on the North African front in 1942. Some Mk VCs did not have all four cannon.

Clipped Spitfire VB (Castle Bromwich-built) of SAAF No. 40 Sqn, on the Italian front in 1943. Note the enlarged 'Aboukir' carburettor-air filter, and the reconnaissance camera behind the cockpit.

Hundreds of Spitfires served in US units, though the XR code on this Castle Bromwich-built Mk VB was originally No. 71 (Eagle) Squadron, RAF, whose pilots were all freelance Americans. EN783 is depicted just after the unit became the 334th Sqn of the USAAF in September 1942.

Another of the 'reverse Lend-Lease' Spitfires was this tropicalised Mk VC, JK226 (Castle Bromwich), assigned to the 308th Fighter Squadron, 31st FG, of the US 12th Air Force in Tunisia.

No. 54 Sqn, RAF, changed its code letters from DL to KL in 1940, but reverted to the original at some point during three months en route to Australia in 1942. By February 1943 it was again in business with tropical Spitfire VCs defending Darwin alongside Nos 452 and 457 Sqns of the RAAF, all under W/C 'Killer' Caldwell. In 1945 it was disbanded, but No. 183 Sqn was renumbered 54.

A Castle Bromwich Spitfire VC with only two cannon fitted, with tropical filter and naval paint scheme after transfer to the Fleet Air Arm as a non-navalised Seafire I for airfield training. No Seafire I was built as such; all were conversions.

Fierce Storms from Hawker

Famed designer Sydney Camm built fighters that were tough (with a few rare exceptions) and eminently serviceable. But the very important Typhoon proved such a disappointment it was almost cancelled, and found its niche as a ground-attack aircraft.

Though a disappointing fighter, the Typhoon eventually found its niche as a ground-attack aircraft with bombs and rockets. This rare colour photograph shows a Mk IB of No. 175 Sqn being bombed up with the short-tail 500-lb (227-kg) version.

Though the evergreen Hurricane remained in production well into 1944, Camm recognised even before the war that in many respects it was of an obsolescent character. By 1937 he was drafting a new fighter with all stressed-skin construction, to be powered by one of the new engines in the 2,000 hp (1492 kW) class. Experience showed that the best engine was an air-cooled radial, the Bristol Centaurus, but the official view was almost to ignore such engines until an example of the superb and radial-engined Focke-Wulf Fw 190 was captured in 1942. So Camm concentrated on the Rolls-Royce Vulture, with 24 cylinders in X-arrangement, and the Napier Sabre, with 24 much smaller cylinders in a unique assemblage resembling two horizontally opposed 12-cylinder units with the upper and lower crankshafts geared to a single front output pinion. The result was the F.18/37 specification to cover the Hawker Tornado (Vulture) and Typhoon (Sabre).

Almost the same size as the Hurricane, these fighters looked much more impressive. The first Tornado flew on 6 October 1939, and the first Typhoon (distinguished by having only one row of exhaust stacks on each side instead of two) followed on 24 February 1940. Eventually the Vulture had to be abandoned, and the Tornado was abandoned with it. This was tragic, because in

One of the last Typhoons to have side doors and a fixed canopy, JR371 is seen bombed-up with No. 198 Sqn, a major constituent unit of the 2nd Tactical Air Force in 1944.

October 1941 a Tornado had flown with a Centaurus, a splendid 18-cylinder sleeve-valve radial, and although the installation was a bit of a lash-up, it did reach 421 mph (678 km/h), faster than any other fighter in the world at that time. The Centaurus continued to be ignored, and every effort was put behind the Typhoon; but the Sabre suffered from such severe troubles that it was officially called 'one of the Second World War's most melancholy stories', and the Centaurus would not fit in the Typhoon airframe.

Though the Typhoon had a modern wing structure, aerodynamically it was on the thick side, and the wing was nothing like as good at high speeds as that of the Spitfire. This caused high drag, which combined with the high wing-loading to give performance far below the predicted values, together with poor manoeuvrability. The cockpit had unusual car-type doors on each side, and in high-speed dives these tended to unlock and try to open because of suction on the external hand-lever. Worse, flutter of the elevators caused persistent failure of the rear fuselage, which added to the casualties from frequent engine failure. Though a few Typhoons reached No.56 Squadron and the Air Fighting Development Unit before the end of 1941, there were so many

An air-to-air photo secured during flight testing from the Gloster factory. The aircraft is a Typhoon IB with bubble canopy.

Fierce Storms from Hawker

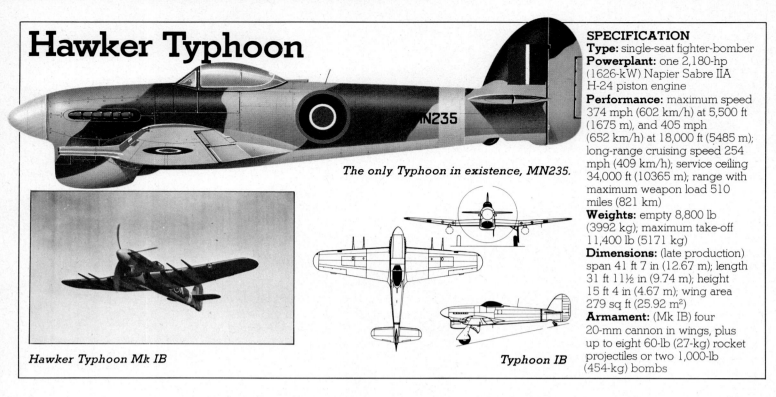

Hawker Typhoon

The only Typhoon in existence, MN235.

Hawker Typhoon Mk IB

Typhoon IB

SPECIFICATION
Type: single-seat fighter-bomber
Powerplant: one 2,180-hp (1626-kW) Napier Sabre IIA H-24 piston engine
Performance: maximum speed 374 mph (602 km/h) at 5,500 ft (1675 m), and 405 mph (652 km/h) at 18,000 ft (5485 m); long-range cruising speed 254 mph (409 km/h); service ceiling 34,000 ft (10365 m); range with maximum weapon load 510 miles (821 km)
Weights: empty 8,800 lb (3992 kg); maximum take-off 11,400 lb (5171 kg)
Dimensions: (late production) span 41 ft 7 in (12.67 m); length 31 ft 11½ in (9.74 m); height 15 ft 4 in (4.67 m); wing area 279 sq ft (25.92 m²)
Armament: (Mk IB) four 20-mm cannon in wings, plus up to eight 60-lb (27-kg) rocket projectiles or two 1,000-lb (454-kg) bombs

A Typhoon development aircraft with the original canopy, long-barrel cannon with fairings, four-blade propeller and several non-standard details. The great effort put into Typhoon development was nullified by inherent shortcomings in altitude performance and, for the first four years, reliability.

problems that for much of 1942 the whole programme was under threat of cancellation. It was only the tenacity and personal example of R.P.Beamont (then CO of No.609 Sqn and later a famed test pilot) that just saved this potentially valuable aircraft.

Low-level potential

Beamont, who had played a major role in the Hawker flight-test programme, could do nothing to give the Typhoon the hoped-for speed or performance at high altitude, but he was convinced that at low levels it was as good as any other fighter and much better than most. In particular he was interested in its performance in the ground-attack role, but first he managed to show its worth as a low-level interceptor of Luftwaffe hit-and-run raiders, mainly Fw 190s, which no other RAF

Early Typhoon IB with car-type doors and fixed canopy, which to some degree spoilt pilot view. Aircraft JG carries the initials of John Grandy, commander of the Duxford Wing in June 1942 (and 20 years later Chief of the Air Staff, retiring as a Marshal of the Royal Air Force).

Typhoon IB DN406 belonged to No. 609 Sqn; on 12 March 1943 it caught and destroyed a lone Fw 190 over Kent, while 18 small white locomotives record confirmed 'kills' over France.

Despite its late serial number, this Typhoon IB has unfaired gun barrels, as well as the original form of cockpit. It is seen with No. 3 Sqn at West Malling, from where it made its last mission on 18 May 1943, being shot down by I/JG27 over Poix airfield.

Typhoon IB MN363 (serial obscured by invasion stripes in June 1944) of No. 247 Sqn, which later became the first to get Vampires.

No. 193 Sqn was one of the intensely active wartime units which had an existence of a bare three years and flew only the Typhoon IB. Under W/C Baldwin several of its aircraft shot up Rommel's staff car, wounding the German C-in-C West.

Hawker Typhoon

This illustration shows a Typhoon IB of the final production standard with bubble hood and four-blade propeller. An aircraft of No. 181 Sqn, it is shown with rockets loaded but without the engine air filter that was urgently fitted in July 1944.

Fierce Storms from Hawker

A brace of fully up-to-date Typhoon IBs, the upper (of No. 175 Sqn, with rockets) being from the final batch (though one could argue JR210 was later, because it was numbered TR210 in error). RB389 served with No. 440 Sqn of the RCAF, and is shown with two 1,000-lb (454-kg) bombs.

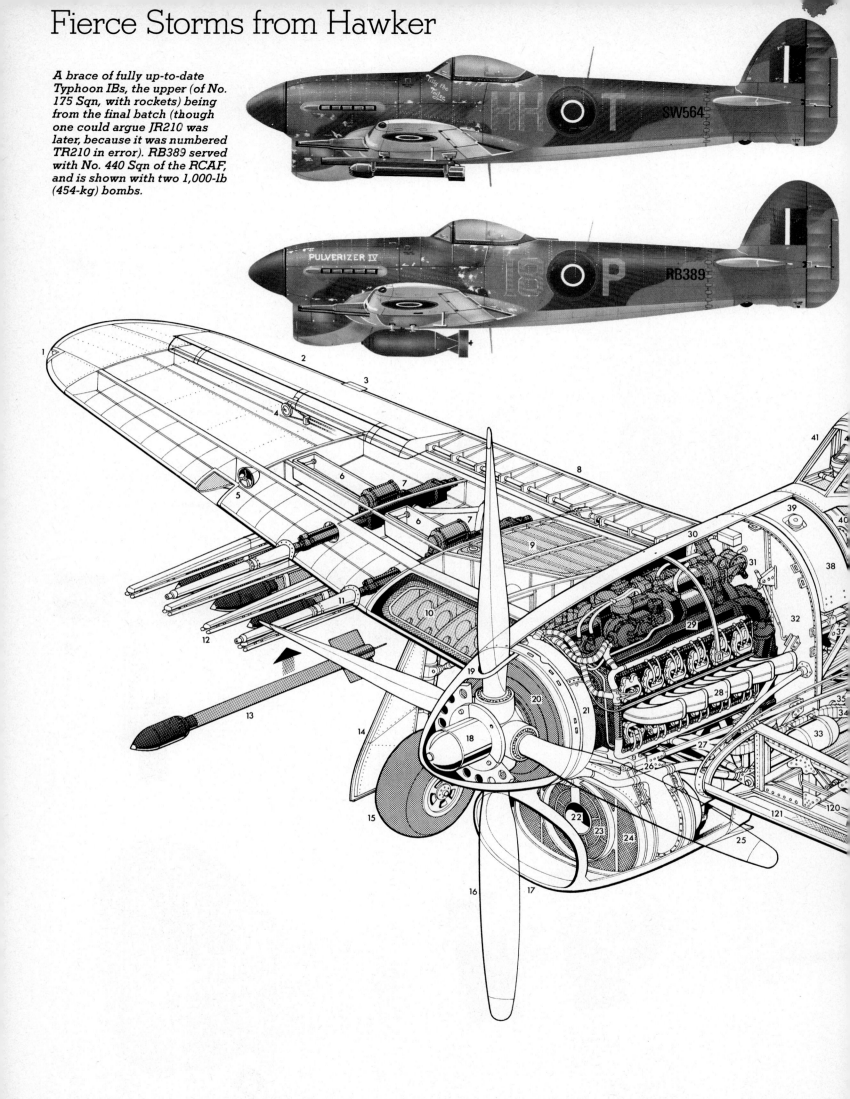

Hawker Typhoon Mk IB cutaway drawing key

1 Starboard navigation light
2 Starboard aileron
3 Fixed trim tab
4 Aileron hinge control
5 Landing lamp
6 Ammunition boxes
7 Starboard 20-mm Hispano Mk II cannon
8 Split trailing edge flaps
9 Starboard main fuel tank, capacity 40 Imp gal (182 litres)
10 Self-sealing leading edge fuel tank, capacity 35 Imp gal (159 litres)
11 Cannon barrel fairings
12 Rocket launcher rails
13 60-lb (27-kg) ground attack rockets
14 Main undercarriage leg fairing

15 Starboard mainwheel
16 De Havilland four-bladed propeller
17 Air intake
18 Propeller pitch change mechanism
19 Spinner
20 Armoured spinner backplate
21 Coolant tank, 7¼ Imp gal (33 litres) capacity
22 Supercharge ram air intake
23 Oil radiator
24 Coolant radiator
25 Radiator shutter
26 Engine mounting block
27 Tubular steel engine support framework
28 Exhaust stubs
29 Napier Sabre II, 24-cylinder flat H engine

30 Engine cowlings
31 Cartridge starter
32 Engine compartment fireproof bulkhead
33 Oxygen bottle
34 Gun heating air duct
35 Hydraulic reservoir
36 Footguards
37 Rudder pedals
38 Oil tank, capacity 18 Imp gal (82 litres)
39 Oil tank filler cap
40 Instrument panel
41 Bullet-proof windscreen
42 Reflector sight
43 Control column handgrip
44 Engine throttle controls
45 Trim handwheels

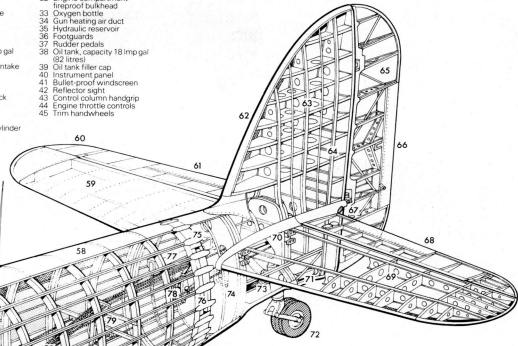

46 Emergency hydraulic handpump
47 Forward fuselage steel tube construction
48 Pilot's seat
49 Safety harness
50 Back and head armour plate
51 Pneumatic system air bottle
52 Rearward sliding canopy cover
53 Aft fuselage joint
54 Canopy rails
55 Radio transmitter/receiver
56 Fuselage double frame
57 Whip aerial
58 Fuselage skinning
59 Starboard tailplane
60 Starboard elevator
61 Elevator trim tab
62 Fin leading edge

63 Fin construction
64 Rudder sternpost
65 Fabric covered rudder construction
66 Rudder trim tab
67 Tail navigation light
68 Elevator trim tab
69 Port tailplane construction
70 Tailplane spar attachments
71 Tailwheel hydraulic jack
72 Forward retracting tailwheel
73 Dowty oleo-pneumatic tailwheel strut
74 Tailplane spar fixing double bulkhead
75 Tailplane attachment joint strap
76 External strengthening fishplates
77 Elevator mass balance
78 Elevator cross shaft
79 Cable guides
80 Tailplane control cables
81 Rear fuselage frame and stringer construction

82 Wing root fillet
83 Spar root pin joints
84 Undercarriage door hydraulic jack
85 Mainwheel door
86 Main undercarriage bay
87 Rear spar
88 Port main fuel tank, capacity 40 Imp gal (182 litres)
89 Flap shroud construction
90 Port split trailing edge flaps
91 Flap hydraulic jack
92 Port gun bays
93 20-mm Hispano Mk II cannon
94 Ammunition feed drum
95 Ammunition boxes, 140 rounds per gun
96 Gun heater air ducts
97 Port aileron
98 Fixed aileron tab
99 Wing tip construction
100 Port navigation light
101 Wing rib construction
102 Wing stringers

103 Front spar
104 Leading edge nose ribs
105 Gun camera
106 Camera port
107 Landing lamp
108 1,000-lb (454-kg) bomb
109 Long range tank, capacity 90 Imp gal (409 litre)
110 Underwing stores pylon
111 Cannon barrel fairings
112 Recoil spring
113 Leading edge construction
114 Main undercarriage leg
115 Undercarriage leg fairing door
116 Oleo-pneumatic shock absorber strut
117 Port mainwheel
118 Undercarriage locking mechanism
119 Mainwheel hydraulic jack
120 Wing spar inboard girder construction
121 Port leading edge fuel tank, capacity 35 Imp gal (159 litres)

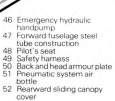

Fierce Storms from Hawker

The bulk of the 800 Tempest Vs were of the Series 2 model whose guns could not be seen. This example from No. 501 (County of Gloucester) AAF squadron has 45-Imp gal (205-litre) drop tanks.

One of the few distinguishing features of the Tempest VI was its oil-cooler and engine-air inlets in the wing roots (because a more powerful Sabre engine needed the whole of the original radiator duct area for cooling). This Mk VI served post-war with No. 213 Sqn, mainly at Shallufa, Egypt.

fighter could easily catch. From November 1942 increasing numbers of Typhoons roamed over Europe by day and night with four 20-mm guns, two 1,000-lb (454-kg) bombs and, from 1943, eight 60-lb (27-kg) rockets. In this role the bluff but capable Typhoon at least found its forté.

Invasion paint scheme

Scramble by Typhoons of No. 56 Sqn, which had converted with some misgivings at Duxford as early as September 1941. Eventually this powerful machine was to make good; 13 years later No. 56 introduced another new fighter, the Swift, which did not.

Altogether the RAF received 3,300 Typhoons built by Gloster plus a handful of the 15 production machines from the parent firm. A few early examples were Mk IAs with 12 machine-guns, but the standard model was the Mk IB with four cannon. During the course of production the original cockpit was replaced by a superior cockpit without doors but with one of the new sliding teardrop canopies, giving all-round view. The cannon barrels were covered by neat fairings and the de Havilland three-blade propeller was replaced by a unit with four blades. The prevailing standard of recognition is indicated by the fact that Typhoons were painted with distinctive black/white stripes to prevent 'confusion with an Fw 190'. By late 1944 Typhoons

Camm later admitted he was strongly influenced by the enormous RAF prejudice against any fighter that did not look like a Spitfire in giving the Tempest elliptical wings. At least it never had to carry identification stripes, though like all Allied invading machines all Tempests wore D-Day stripes from 6 June 1944. This aircraft of No. 274 Sqn had them on the underside of the fuselage only.

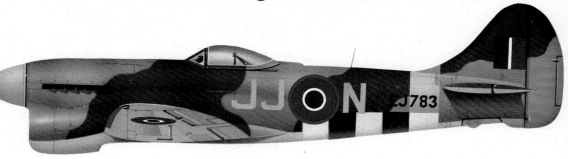

The first Tempests to go into action flew with R.P. Beamont's Newchurch (Kent) Wing, comprising Nos 3 and 486 Sqns from April 1944, with No. 56 Sqn completing the wing in July. From mid-June they were top scorers in intercepting V-1 flying bombs; this No. 486 Sqn machine has two kills.

equipped 23 squadrons in the 2nd Tactical Air Force operating from bases on the continent, and they did more than any other single type to smash the German army in the west.

In 1941 Camm had schemed a Typhoon Mk II with a thinner wing to try to recover some of the lost performance. It was arranged to house four cannon installed farther back, with shorter barrels wholly inside the wing, and this led to a curious elliptical wing plan rather like that of the Spitfire. There was at this time an amazingly powerful prejudice against fighters that did not look like a Spitfire (to the extent that early Typhoon squadrons had to be based at airfields without Spitfire squadrons), and Camm admitted this played a part in deciding the new wing shape! Wisely the Typhoon Mk II was planned to have the Centaurus or Griffon as alternatives to the Sabre, but the first examples had Sabres. The first to fly, HM595 on 2 September 1942, had a Typhoon engine installation with radiator in the chin position, but the next machine, in February 1943, had wing leading-edge radiators and achieved 466 mph (750 km/h). Eventually the aircraft was renamed Tempest and put into production with the original engine installation as the Mk V; even so, it was not only much faster than a Typhoon but more manoeuvrable, and a most formidable fighter except at high altitude.

A regular production Tempest, one of a batch of 130 Mk V Series 2 with spring-tab ailerons and gun barrels wholly within the wings.

Fierce Storms from Hawker

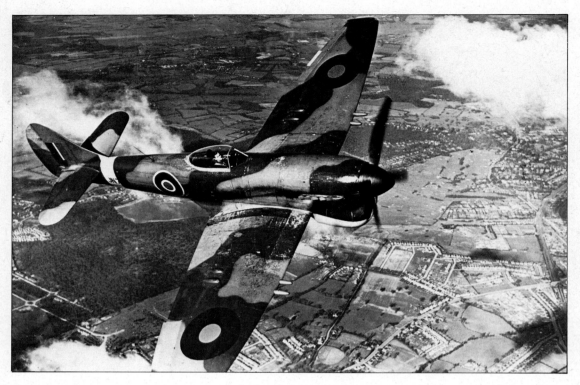

One of the first production Tempests (the first was JN729) on test from Langley in June 1943. The initial batches were called Tempest V Series 1; the main run of Series 2 had Hispano Mk V cannon with short barrels which did not project ahead of the leading edge, and rate of roll was improved by fitting spring-tab ailerons.

Both Hawker and Gloster made Tempests, and they were the top scoring killers of V-1 flying bombs in the summer and autumn of 1944, besides establishing complete superiority over the Luftwaffe — to a remarkable degree this even extended to the Messerschmitt Me 262 jet, though the Me 262 was almost 100 mph (161 km/h) faster. The Tempest Mk V series 2 had slightly more power, spring-tab ailerons for faster rate of roll and short barrel Mk V cannon wholly buried in the wings.

Cancelled variants

Two even better Tempests failed to reach the RAF until after the war. One was the Mk VI, with a more powerful version of the Sabre and the oil cooler displaced to the right wing, with small inlet

PR533 was one of the first of 332 Tempest II fighters built by Hawker at Langley. Certainly the best of all the wartime Hawker fighters, the Mk II was tragically subjected to prolonged delays, mainly because of official disbelief that an air-cooled engine could prove suitable. When a Centaurus was installed by Camm in the prototype Typhoon II (thin-wing, later named Tempest) in August 1942, Air Marshal Freeman ordered the engine removed. This aircraft was thereby delayed a full year.

Hawker Tempest

SPECIFICATION

Type: single-seat fighter/fighter-bomber

Powerplant: (Mk V) one 2,180-hp (1626-kW) Napier Sabre IIA H-24 piston engine

Performance: maximum speed 426 mph (686 km/h) at 18,500 ft (5640 m); service ceiling 36,500 ft (11125 m); maximum range 1,530 miles (2462 km)

Weights: empty 9,000 lb (4082 kg); maximum take-off 13,540 lb (6142 kg)

Dimensions: span 41 ft 0 in (12.50 m); length 33 ft 8 in (10.26 m); height 16 ft 1 in (4.90 m)

Armament: four 20-mm cannon, plus two 500-lb (227-kg) or two 1,000-lb (454-kg) bombs, or eight 60-lb (27-kg) rocket projectiles

Tempest II seen in service with the first recipient, No. 183 Sqn, which was renumbered No. 54 Sqn before being declared operational.

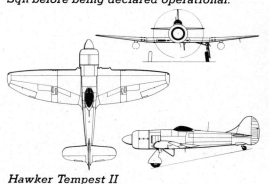

Hawker Tempest II

Hawker Tempest V

ducts at the root on each side to serve the engine's injection carburettor. Napier tested lower-drag Sabre installations with annular radiators, either with a conventional propeller or with a large ducted spinner giving an appearance like a jet aircraft, but these did not go into production. The best Tempest of all was powered by the shamefully neglected Centaurus radial. This Mk II aircraft flew as a prototype at Langley on 28 June 1943. It was also ordered from Gloster in 1942 but severely delayed by Gloster's overwork; eventually the programme was moved to the Bristol Aeroplane Company, where at last a Tempest Mk II flew on 4 October 1944. The programme was then moved back to Hawker, so that this first-class fighter-bomber missed the war, Bristol actually making 50 of the total of 452. Quieter and less-tiring to fly than the Sabre versions, the Mk II was the only mark to remain in the RAF as a fighter after the war. From it Hawker derived the Fury and Sea Fury.

The official caption to this photograph states that these Tempests are returning at 10,000 ft (3050 m) from attacking surface targets east of the Rhine. Drop tanks still in place suggests no bombs or rockets were used, and no enemy aircraft sighted.

Fierce Storms from Hawker

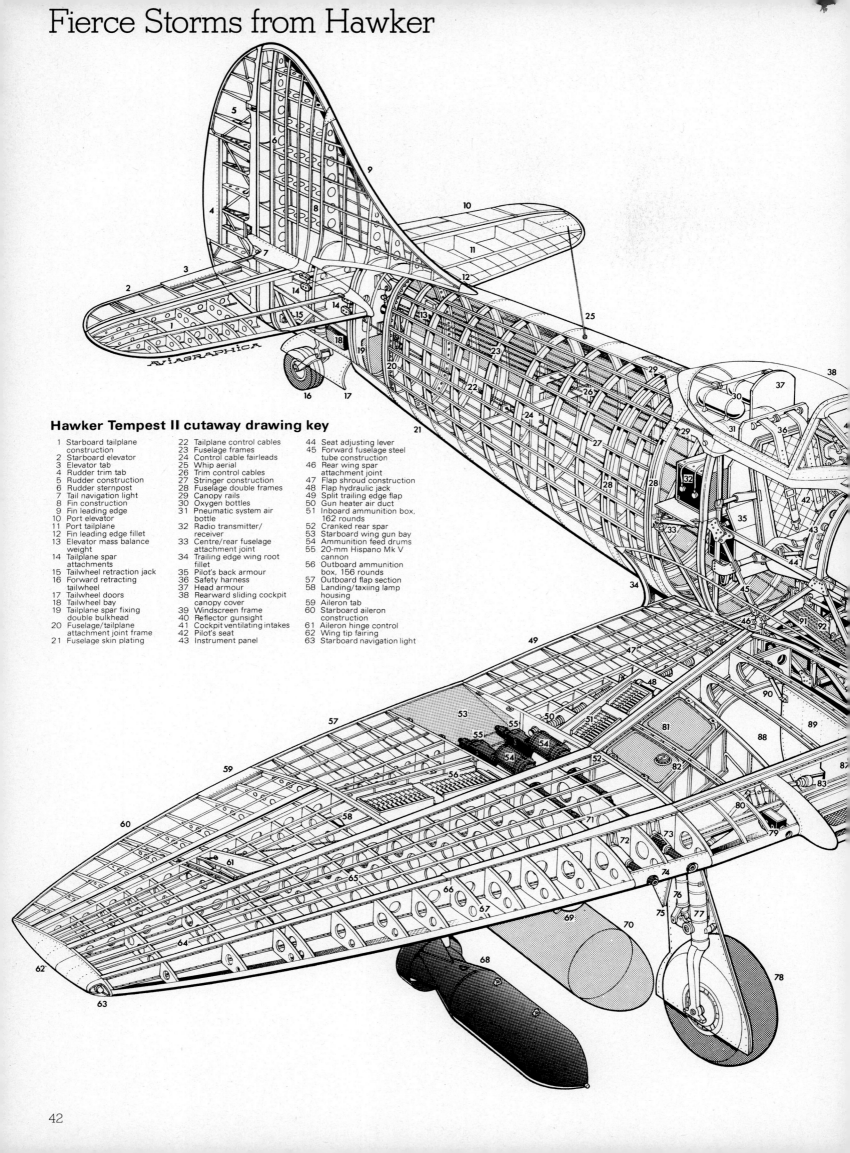

Hawker Tempest II cutaway drawing key

1 Starboard tailplane construction
2 Starboard elevator
3 Elevator tab
4 Rudder trim tab
5 Rudder construction
6 Rudder sternpost
7 Tail navigation light
8 Fin construction
9 Fin leading edge
10 Port elevator
11 Port tailplane
12 Fin leading edge fillet
13 Elevator mass balance weight
14 Tailplane spar attachments
15 Tailwheel retraction jack
16 Forward retracting tailwheel
17 Tailwheel doors
18 Tailwheel bay
19 Tailplane spar fixing double bulkhead
20 Fuselage/tailplane attachment joint frame
21 Fuselage skin plating

22 Tailplane control cables
23 Fuselage frames
24 Control cable fairleads
25 Whip aerial
26 Trim control cables
27 Stringer construction
28 Fuselage double frames
29 Canopy rails
30 Oxygen bottles
31 Pneumatic system air bottle
32 Radio transmitter/receiver
33 Centre/rear fuselage attachment joint
34 Trailing edge wing root fillet
35 Pilot's back armour
36 Safety harness
37 Head armour
38 Rearward sliding cockpit canopy cover
39 Windscreen frame
40 Reflector gunsight
41 Cockpit ventilating intakes
42 Pilot's seat
43 Instrument panel

44 Seat adjusting lever
45 Forward fuselage steel tube construction
46 Rear wing spar attachment joint
47 Flap shroud construction
48 Flap hydraulic jack
49 Split trailing edge flap
50 Gun heater air duct
51 Inboard ammunition box, 162 rounds
52 Cranked rear spar
53 Starboard wing gun bay
54 Ammunition feed drums
55 20-mm Hispano Mk V cannon
56 Outboard ammunition box, 156 rounds
57 Outboard flap section
58 Landing/taxiing lamp housing
59 Aileron tab
60 Starboard aileron construction
61 Aileron hinge control
62 Wing tip fairing
63 Starboard navigation light

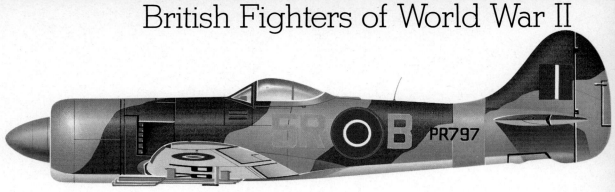

The squadron commander of No. 33 Sqn flew this Tempest II (post-war styled F.2) in Germany and, from 1949, in Hong Kong and Malaya. In 1951 it was the last surviving Tempest squadron.

64 Wing stringer construction
65 Wing ribs
66 Front spar
67 Leading edge nose ribs
68 1,000-lb (454-kg) bomb
69 Underwing stores pylon
70 Drop tank, capacity 45 Imp gal (205 litres)
71 Cannon barrels

72 Cannon barrel front mounting
73 Recoil spring housing
74 Cannon muzzles
75 Main undercarriage leg doors
76 Shock absorber strut
77 Levered suspension main undercarriage leg
78 Starboard mainwheel

79 Gun camera
80 Undercarriage retraction linkage
81 Starboard wing fuel tank, capacity 28 Imp gal (127 litres)
82 Fuel filler cap
83 Undercarriage hydraulic jack
84 Oil radiator
85 Ram air intake

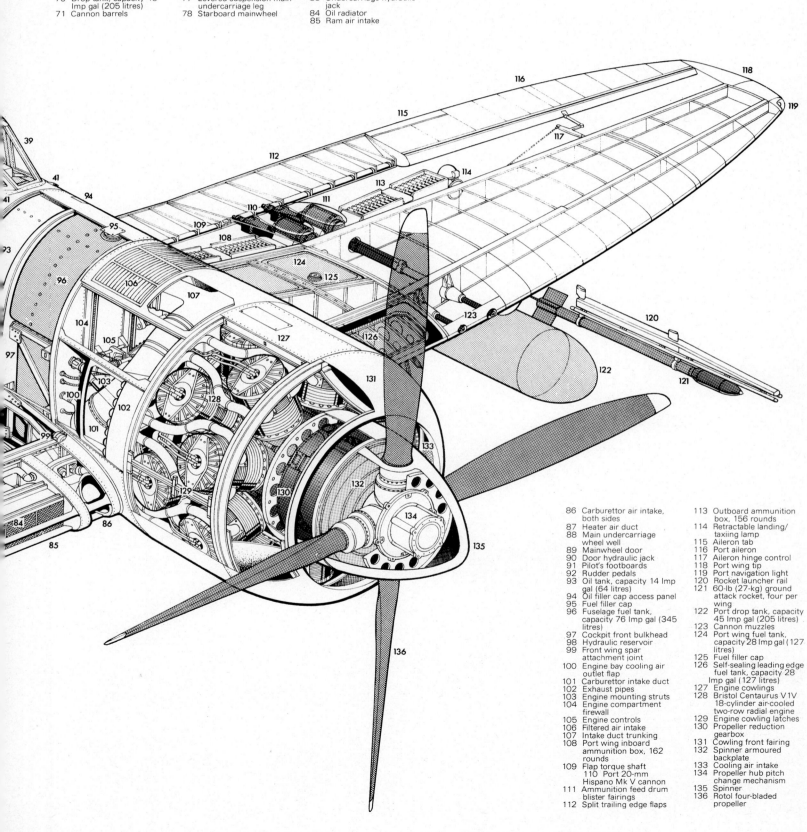

86 Carburettor air intake, both sides
87 Heater air duct
88 Main undercarriage wheel well
89 Mainwheel door
90 Door hydraulic jack
91 Pilot's footboards
92 Rudder pedals
93 Oil tank, capacity 14 Imp gal (64 litres)
94 Oil filler cap access panel
95 Fuel filler cap
96 Fuselage fuel tank, capacity 76 Imp gal (345 litres)
97 Cockpit front bulkhead
98 Hydraulic reservoir
99 Front wing spar attachment joint
100 Engine bay cooling air outlet flap
101 Carburettor intake duct
102 Exhaust pipes
103 Engine mounting struts
104 Engine compartment firewall
105 Engine controls
106 Filtered air intake
107 Intake duct trunking
108 Port wing inboard ammunition box, 162 rounds
109 Flap torque shaft
110 Port 20-mm Hispano Mk V cannon
111 Ammunition feed drum blister fairings
112 Split trailing edge flaps

113 Outboard ammunition box, 156 rounds
114 Retractable landing/taxiing lamp
115 Aileron tab
116 Port aileron
117 Aileron hinge control
118 Port wing tip
119 Port navigation light
120 Rocket launcher rail
121 60-lb (27-kg) ground attack rocket, four per wing
122 Port drop tank, capacity 45 Imp gal (205 litres)
123 Cannon muzzles
124 Port wing fuel tank, capacity 28 Imp gal (127 litres)
125 Fuel filler cap
126 Self-sealing leading edge fuel tank, capacity 28 Imp gal (127 litres)
127 Engine cowlings
128 Bristol Centaurus V1V 18-cylinder air-cooled two-row radial engine
129 Engine cowling latches
130 Propeller reduction gearbox
131 Cowling front fairing
132 Spinner armoured backplate
133 Cooling air intake
134 Propeller hub pitch change mechanism
135 Spinner
136 Rotol four-bladed propeller

Later Spitfires

Under Joe Smith's direction the Spitfire was developed to such a degree that the later Griffon-engined versions had practically nothing in common with the Mk I. They were among the best piston-engined fighters ever built.

While the Spitfire V was basically a strengthened Mk I with a more powerful Merlin engine, the Mk IX was just a hasty lash-up of the Mk V with the new 60-series Merlin giving much greater high-altitude performance, yet it was kept in production until 5,739 had been built! These Mk IXs were patrolling over Anzio in January 1944.

Though the Spitfire ran up a string of mark numbers as high as 24, virtually all were production types. There were remarkably few oddities or unsuccessful versions, or even experimental fits of equipment or armament. Amazingly, though there were schemes for several others, no engine was fitted except the regular Merlin or Griffon (apart from two trial installations of the Daimler Benz DB 601 and 605 on Spitfires captured by the Germans). The only markedly different proposal was for a so-called 'Plastic Spitfire' with a high proportion of resin-bonded flax and wood construction, and though it would have achieved its objective of conserving imported aluminium it was never built.

The mass-produced Mk V has already been described, as a Mk I or II with more power. The Mk III would have introduced further improvements, including wheels set further forward to avoid nosing-over, the bullet-proof windscreen inside instead of outside, better armour protection and a retractable tailwheel, but only two were made. The mark number IV was confusingly used twice. The PR.IV was just an unarmed photo-reconnaissance Mk V, but the true Mk IV was the first of a completely different family with the larger Griffon engine. The Mk IV, DP845, was a frequently modified aircraft with four-blade propeller and retractable tailwheel, and it had six cannon.

The Mk VI was the first special high-altitude model, with a pressurised cockpit without side

access flaps and with a special non-sliding hood. Long-span pointed wings were fitted, and the engine was a Merlin 47 driving a four-blade propeller; otherwise the 100 delivered were like Mk Vs. The slightly improved engine and extended tips raised service ceiling considerably, but a far greater improvement came with the Merlin 60-series engine, which had two superchargers in series and an intercooler. Installation of this new family of engines was signalled by a longer nose, six exhaust stubs on each side, four-blade propeller and symmetrical cooling radiators, one under each wing. The first Spitfire to have one of these engines, which doubled the power available above 30,000 ft (9145 m), was the Mk VII. This was a most effective high-altitude fighter, with pointed wings, retractable tailwheel, pressurised cockpit and a broad pointed rudder also flown at this time (April 1942) on the Mk XII.

Just as the 6,479 Mk Vs were mere re-engined lash-ups of the original Spitfire, so was the next most numerous mark, the 5,739 Mk IXs, merely a hasty re-engined lash-up of the Mk V. There has never been any attempt to explain why the Mk IX was kept in production almost to the end of the war in preference to the intended model, the Mk VIII. The Mk IX was rushed through to meet the severe challenge of the Fw 190 in 1942. It was basically a Mk V with the Merlin 61; indeed

If the Spitfire had a serious shortcoming it was inadequate fuel capacity, but the dedicated photo-reconnaissance marks went some way to rectifying this. By far the most important was the PR.XI, seen here with Invasion Stripes, which covered targets east of Berlin and in Poland and Czechoslovakia.

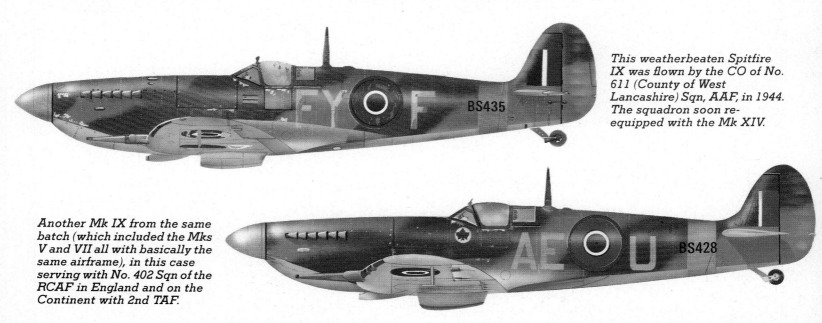

This weatherbeaten Spitfire IX was flown by the CO of No. 611 (County of West Lancashire) Sqn, AAF, in 1944. The squadron soon re-equipped with the Mk XIV.

Another Mk IX from the same batch (which included the Mks V and VII all with basically the same airframe), in this case serving with No. 402 Sqn of the RCAF in England and on the Continent with 2nd TAF.

Supermarine Spitfire IX

SPECIFICATION

Type: single-seat day fighter-bomber

Powerplant: one 1,515-hp (1130-kW) Rolls-Royce Merlin 61 or 1,710-hp (1276-kW) Merlin 63 or 63A V-12 piston engine

Performance: maximum speed 408 mph (657 km/h) at 25,000 ft (7620 m); service ceiling 44,000 ft (13410 m); range on internal fuel 434 miles (698 km)

Weights: empty 5,610 lb (2545 kg); maximum take-off 7,500 lb (3402 kg)

Dimensions: span (normal) 36 ft 10 in (11.23 m), (clipped) 32 ft 2 in or 32 ft 7 in (9.93 m); length 31 ft 3½ in (9.54 m); height 11 ft 9 in (3.58 m); wing area (normal) 242 sq ft (22.48 m²), (clipped) 231.0 sq ft (21.46 m²)

Spitfire F.IX of No. 340 (Free French) Sqn, RAF. Note the Cross of Lorraine, the insignia of the Free French forces.

Armament: two 20-mm Hispano cannon and either four 0.303-in (7.7-mm) machine guns or (E-type wing) two 20-mm and two 0.50-in (12.7-mm) and provision for up to 1,000-lb (454-kg) bombload (two 250-lb/113-kg) under wings and one 500-lb/227-kg under fuselage)

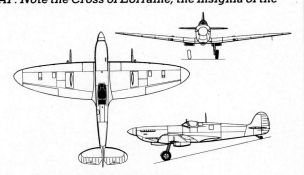

Supermarine Spitfire F.IX

The RAF and Royal Navy never had a water-based fighter in World War 2, though Folland Aircraft tested a seaplane conversion of a Spitfire VB in 1942 and this broadly similar conversion of a Mk IX in 1943. Note the extra fin area needed by this rebuild, which was successful but never put into production.

hundreds began life as the earlier version and were fitted with the new engine either on the assembly line or after delivery. Though unpressurised, some Mk IXs had the long-span pointed wing, while a much larger number had the LF (low-altitude fighter) clipped wing. Most had the B-wing with two cannon. By 1944 the E-wing was also common, with two cannon and two 0.5-in (12.7-mm) heavy machine-guns. As on the other marks a flush-fitting slipper drop tank of 45, 90 or (rarely) 170 Imp gal (205, 409 or 773 litres) could be fitted under the belly; alternatively a 500-lb (227-kg) bomb could be hung here, plus two 250-lb (113-kg) bombs under the wings. Other features included a broader rudder, sometimes with the pointed top, and metal-skinned ailerons.

The very last batches of Mk IXs had a teardrop hood, and this was also a feature of the Mk XVI, mass-produced from 1944 at Castle Bromwich as a Mk IX with the American-made Packard Merlin 266. Most of this series were of the LF.XVIE type, with clipped wings and E-type guns.

Supermarine Spitfire VII

SPECIFICATION

Type: single-seat high-altitude interceptor

Powerplant: (F.VII) one 1,710-hp (1276-kW) Rolls-Royce Merlin 64 V-12 piston engine

Performance: maximum speed 408 mph (657 km/h) at 25,000 ft (7620 m); maximum cruising speed 324 mph (521 km/h) at 20,000 ft (6095 m); service ceiling 43,000 ft (13105 m); range (internal fuel) 660 miles (1062 km), (with maximum external fuel) 1,180 miles (1899 km)

Weights: empty 6,000 lb (2722 kg); maximum take-off 7,875 lb (3572 kg)

Dimensions: span 40 ft 2 in (12.24 m); length 31 ft 3½ in (9.54 m); height 11 ft 8½ in (3.57 m); wing area 248.5 sq ft

This Spitfire F.VII was painted medium sea grey and PRU blue, with B-type insignia, and served with No. 131 Sqn.

(23.09 m²)
Armament: two 20-mm Hispano cannon and four 0.303-in (7.7-mm) Browning machine-guns

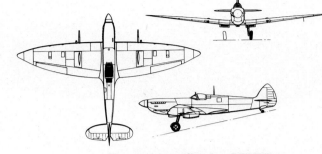

Supermarine Spitfire HF.VII.

After the war they were redesignated Mk 16.

Thus, while floods of lash-up Mk IX and Mk XVI Spitfires were made, the parent firm slowly proceeded with the intended variant with the Merlin 60-series engine, the Mk VIII. This had many refinements such as all those introduced on the Mk VII except pressurisation, and a Universal wing able to take any armament and have any span, with short-span metal ailerons. The Mk VIII was certainly the nicest of all marks to fly, but Supermarine got into real production only in mid-1943 and a mere 1,658 were built, all being tropicalised and sent overseas. The Mk VIII was the chief variant in the Pacific theatre.

Photo-recce variants

By far the best of many photo-reconnaissance versions was the PR.XI, basically a Mk VIII with guns removed, leading-edge fuel tanks, an enlarged oil tank (resulting in a characteristically deep underside to the cowling) for missions lasting up to 10 hours, and comprehensive camera installations. The Mk XI frequently went on lone missions to places as distant as Berlin and Prague, with no special navigation aids or electronic defence. The PR.XIII was a low-level reconnaissance rebuild of the Mk V, 18 being converted with a Merlin 32 and four-blade propeller; unusually among PR variants, they had four machine-guns.

DP845, the Mk IV already mentioned, was redesignated Mk XX and finally, in early 1942,

This aircraft, DP845, was retained by Supermarine and Rolls-Royce for prolonged research and passed through numerous contrasting forms. It is seen as the first 'Spit' with a Griffon engine, and after being styled Mk IV (there was already a PR.IV with a Merlin) was designated Spitfire XX. Chief test pilot Jeffery Quill thought it the best Spitfire to fly, though one had to remember the propeller rotated in the opposite direction, so swing on take-off was not to the left but to the right.

Later Spitfires

Generally agreed to be the nicest of all marks to fly, the Mk VIII had all the refinements lacking in the Mk IX and was intended to be the standard production model from late 1942, but was delayed by repeated re-orders for the Mk IX. This Mk VIII served with the USAAF 31st Fighter Group on the Italian front in 1944.

This extremely rare bird was originally one of the earliest Spitfire I fighters ordered in 1937 and delivered just after the outbreak of war. It is shown as a Type C photo-reconnaissance conversion (the basis for the later PR.IV), assigned to Photo Reconnaissance Unit Detachment E (Experimental) under F/Lt 'Shorty' Longbottom in August 1940. One of the unit's tasks was selecting a colour scheme for low and high photo missions.

The Soviet Union received 1,188 Mk IX Spitfires, though like most supplies from Western Allies they appear to have been under-utilised. Some, such as this black-painted example, were locally converted as high-speed liaison aircraft without guns. Others were dual trainers, a type missing from the RAF.

Named for a dangerous type of shark, this Mk VIII was flown by WC Glenn Cooper, CO of No. 457 Sqn, RAAF. As a newly re-formed unit with totally raw pilots it helped defend Darwin in 1942-3 but later, with the Spitfire VIII, it became highly offensive.

By far the most important reconnaissance Spitfire version was the Mk XI, designed from the start for such duty and with extra fuel in the wing in place of guns. The longer duration of flights as far as Berlin and Prague demanded more engine oil, hence the deeper cowling. Other features included a simple (not bullet-proof) windscreen and retractable tailwheel. Not all had a pointed rudder.

TZ214 was an FR.XVIII serving in the Middle East with No. 32 Sqn. This mark resembled the FR.XIV with teardrop hood but had a stronger wing and landing gear, extra fuel (both in the wings and rear fuselage) and normal, instead of clipped, wingtips.

The last mark to enter service in wartime was the completely redesigned F.21, which reached No. 91 Sqn at West Malling in March 1945. As this aircraft from that squadron shows, it still lacked the teardrop hood and cut-down rear fuselage, introduced on the Mk 22 later in 1945.

Supermarine Spitfire XIV

SPECIFICATION
Type: single-seat interceptor fighter/fighter-bomber
Powerplant: (Mk XIV) one 2,050-hp (1529-kW) Rolls-Royce Griffon 65 V-12 piston engine
Performance: maximum speed 448 mph (721 km/h) at 26,000 ft (7925 m); cruising speed 362 mph (583 km/h); service ceiling 43,000 ft (13105 m); range 850 miles (1368 km) with maximum auxiliary fuel
Weights: empty 6,700 lb (3039 kg); maximum take-off 10,280 lb (4663 kg)
Dimensions: span 36 ft 10 in (11.23 m); length 32 ft 8 in (3.86 m); wing area 244 sq ft (22.67 m²)
Armament: two 20-mm cannon and two 0.50-in (12.7-mm) machine-guns

This Spitfire Mk XIV was flown by S/L R.A. Newbury, CO of No. 610 Sqn chasing flying bombs while based at Lympne.

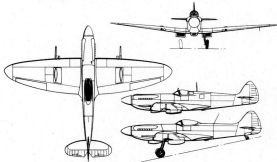

Supermarine Spitfire F.XIVE

Spitfire XIV.

became the basis for the Mk XII, the first production Spitfire with the larger Griffon engine. The Mk XII was, like the Mk V and MK IX, a hasty lash-up, in this case to chase low-level Fw 190s bombing southern England. Thus the low-rated Griffon III or VI, with four-blade propeller, was ideal to pull what was otherwise basically an LF.Mk V at high speed at low level. Only 100 were built, in 1942, the final 45 being based on the Mk VII and thus having the broad pointed rudder and retractable tailwheel. These were the first of the Griffon Spitfires, a totally different breed with a different set of flight characteristics. On take-off, for example, the Mk XII swung violently to the right (unless the rudder was trimmed hard-left) instead of more gently to the left.

Greater power at higher altitude

Rolls-Royce developed the Griffon as they had the Merlin, and with the 60-series introduced a two-stage supercharger and intercooler to give very much greater power at all levels, and almost double at high altitudes. The result was the most formidable of all Spitfires to see widespread war service, the Mk XIV. This was a Mk VIII, or late Mk XII, with the great Griffon 65, resulting in an even longer nose than that of the Mk XII and needing a five-blade propeller to absorb the power of well over 2,000 hp (1492 kW). To counter the destabilising effect of the long nose, the fin and rudder were further increased in chord, and to cool the engine symmetric radiator and oil cooler ducts, of much greater depth than those of the Mk IX, were fitted. The wing was a Universal (E) or C, the latter having the cannon in the outer instead of the inner positions and for the first time being wired for rocket projectiles. The 957 built included many FR.XIVEs with clipped wings and oblique cameras in a cut-down rear fuselage for a teardrop hood, which reduced directional stability close to zero.

At the end of the war the standard fighter mark being delivered was the Mk XVIII, basically a

Typical of late-wartime production, this Spitfire was built as an FR.XIV with a reconnaissance camera behind the cockpit, and with the teardrop canopy and cut-down rear fuselage. Later the camera was removed, turning it into an F.14 in post-war parlance, and it was given to No. 6 Sqn of the Indian Air Force.

This was the last Spitfire to make an operational flight with the RAF. The date was 1 April 1954, and it was a PR.19 of No. 81 Sqn in Malaya.

Later Spitfires

The Royal Auxiliary Air Force used late-mark Spitfires after the war. No. 602 (City of Glasgow) squadron, which had used the old Mk V right up to March 1944, briefly used the Mks IX and XVI and then went on to Griffons, this Mk 21 being one of nine used in 1947.

Though unmistakably Spitfires, these Mk 21s have hardly a single part common to any of the Merlin-engined versions, and in particular introduced a completely redesigned wing. In turn this type served as the basis for even more advanced marks of Seafire.

refined Mk XIV with a strengthened airframe, increased internal tankage and standard teardrop hood/cut-down rear fuselage. The FR.XVIII had cameras in place of the added rear-fuselage tanks. Biggest fuel capacity of all was boasted by the similar PR.XIX, which at the end of the war was replacing the Mk XI. Despite its higher fuel consumption, with a two-stage Griffon 66, the Mk XIX had even greater range than the Mk XI, as well as increased altitude and speed. After the war the two-stage Griffon machines remained in service, restyled Mks 14, 18 and 19, and it was a Mk 19 that made the RAF's last Spitfire sortie, in Malaya on 1 April 1954.

The Spitfire Mks 21, 22 and 24 were largely redesigned aircraft, with different wings and even further increased weight and four cannon armament. Prototypes flew from 1944 onwards, but they were essentially post-war versions. With Seafires, discussed in the next chapter, they brought total production up to 22,890.

Naval Fighters

Most British naval fighters were totally outclassed by the Bf 109 and Fw 190 and could barely defeat the earlier Italian fighters. Only in the final year of the war did good Seafires and two-seat Fireflies get into action.

The Fairey Firefly was a most valuable aircraft which only scratched the surface of its capabilities during World War II and went on to fly many other types of mission into the 1960s. This is an early Mk I.

From 1918 until July 1937 the Royal Navy's Fleet Air Arm was a foolishly divided service, the RAF having control of design and provision of aircraft, even the embarked FAA Flights being RAF units, with the light-blue service also providing one-third of the pilots. Carrier-based aircraft are more difficult to design than land-based ones, but the FAA's fighters in 1937 were outdated into the bargain. At the start of the war there were just two types that might be called fighters. One was the excellent Sea Gladiator, a normal Gladiator with catapult hooks, an arrester hook and a belly fairing covering a dinghy. The other was the Blackburn Skua, a trim but underpowered monoplane designed to combine the duties of dive bomber and fighter, and with an observer in the rear cockpit. Right up to the 1960s the Admirality stuck to the belief that seagoing fighters had to have a backseater to do the navigation, and in World War II this made purpose-designed naval fighters slow and unwieldy, and likely to lose any engagement with a land-based single-seater. The Skua did have four forward-firing machine-guns, and gained the UK's first fighter victory of the war (over a Dornier Do 18), but it was quite outclassed as a fighter. A turret-armed development, the Roc, was even more useless; a seaplane version was unable to exceed 178 mph (286 km/h).

Naval Fighters

Presenting a puzzle to the spotter, this Canadian Car & Foundry-built Hurricane X was painted in FAA colours and given an arrester hook as a Sea Hurricane IB, though differing in detail from most of that mark. It was then reassigned for day use with No. 440 Sqn of the RCAF. Note the green obliteration of the words ROYAL NAVY.

In the early war years there was only one British naval fighter worth having, and that had been designed as a land-based bomber! The Fairey Fulmar had a long rear cockpit canopy for the observer, and of necessity was larger than single-seaters; and its weight was increased by folding wings 'and the strength needed for catapult launches and arrested landings. It had eight machine-guns in the folding outer wings, and handled superbly; with a 2,000-hp (1492-kW) engine it would have been a pretty good fighter, but with an early Merlin of half this power it was pure flying skill that brought victories over the Bf 109, and nearly all its successes were gained in the Mediterranean theatre against Italian aircraft. Total production was 600.

Many Fulmars served aboard CAM (catapult-armed merchantman) ships, shot off to fend off Luftwaffe Focke-Wulf Fw 200s and Junkers Ju 88s, afterwards ditching in the sea. The chief CAM fighter was the Hurricane, and from 1941 several marks of fully navalised Sea Hurricane served aboard carriers in a more normal mode in which the fighter was (hopefully) recovered after each mission. None had folding wings, and though useful they were strictly interim machines. Hawker never built the planned carrier-based Typhoon or Tempest, and the ultimate piston fighter, the Sea Fury, was post-war.

Spitfire at sea

By far the most important British naval fighters of World War II were the Seafires. Mitchell had studied a naval Spitfire back in 1936, but no interest was shown until in 1941 the need was urgent (though the tough Grumman Wildcat, an American import at the time called the Martlet, gave the FAA some air-combat capability). For a start about 100 Spitfire Mk VBs were transferred to the FAA and served at RN air stations ashore. Many were fitted with hooks and used for deck training. Then AST (Air Service Training) at Hamble rebuilt about 100 Spitfire Mk Vs (nearly all of them Mk VBs) as the first true Seafires, with mark number IB. They had catapult spools, hooks,

As the Royal Navy's first operational monoplane the Skua had to overcome much doubt and prejudice. Sadly, its poor performance made it almost useless as a fighter, though one did achieve the first British air combat victory of the war.

Fairey Fulmar

SPECIFICATION

Type: two-seat carrier-based fighter

Powerplant: (Mk I) one 1,080-hp (805-kW) Rolls-Royce Merlin VII V-12 piston engine

Performance: maximum speed 247 mph (398 km/h) at 9,000 ft (2745 m); service ceiling 21,500 ft (6555 m); patrol endurance 4 hours with reserves; range 800 miles (1287 km)

Weights: empty 8,720 lb (3955 kg); maximum take-off 10,700 lb (4853 kg)

Dimensions: span 46 ft 4½ in (14.14 m); length 40 ft 2 in (12.24 m); height 14 ft 0 in (4.27 m); wing area 342 sq ft (31.77 m²)

Armament: eight 0.303-in (7.7-mm) machine-guns in wings

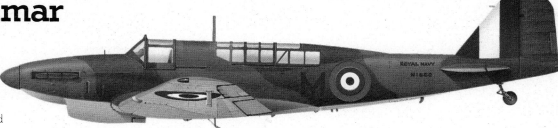

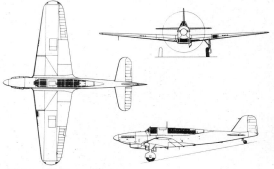

Fairey Fulmar of the Royal Navy engaged in the Mediterranean theatre, 1942.

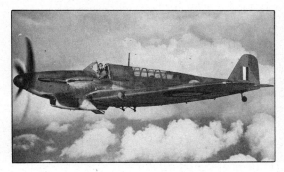

Fairey Fulmar II

naval radio and other equipment, and equipped No. 807 Sqn in June 1942. The first victories were gained against French fighters over Algeria in November 1942. Next came the Seafire Mk IIC, with Universal wing, basic Spitfire Mk VC airframe with local strengthening, and various low-blown engines, the most powerful being of over 1,600 hp (1194 kW) and driving a four-blade propeller. These led to the chief wartime variant, the Seafire Mk III, the first with folding wings. The wings were pushed upwards manually, the tips folding down to reduce height. The Merlin 32 or 55 drove a four-blade propeller, and as in the case of the Mk IIC a proportion were completed as camera-equipped reconnaissance machines. Cunliffe-Owen Aircraft delivered 350 Seafire Mk IIIs and Westland another 870, and these saw action on many fronts, especially at the Salerno landings where they were the only Allied airpower during the first four crucial days.

To avoid confusion Spitfire mark numbers were not repeated in Seafires, so the next was the Mk XV. This was a great advance, for it had a low-blown single-stage Griffon and was in many

A rare high-quality wartime colour photograph showing a Sea Hurricane IB, the first British wartime naval fighter that could actually go to sea and make some impression on the enemy. Most of these early machines were converted RAF Hurricanes, often with a long record of combat duty. This example has added plates ahead of the cockpit to shield the pilot's eyes from exhaust flames at night.

The Seafire III was basically a Spitfire IIC with a Merlin 32 or 55 giving high power at low level, driving a four-blade propeller, and with wings folded upwards just inboard of the guns and braced by telescopic jury struts fitted after landing. The tips folded to give adequate clearance in RN carrier hangars.

ways like a navalised Spitfire Mk XII. Deck landing was improved by switching from the A-frame hook to the US-style sting hook at the base of the rudder. Four FAA squadrons had formed and were working up when the European war ended, but Griffon Seafires just saw action in the Far East. Cunliffe-Owen built 134 Mk XVs and Westland a further 256, and the two companies followed with 189 Mk XVIIs with a cut-down rear fuselage, teardrop canopy and increased internal fuel. By 1945 far more powerful two-stage Griffon Seafires were flying, culminating with the great Mk 47 which was the ultimate member of the Spitfire/Seafire family and fought in Korea.

Fairey's Firefly

Urgency was missing from the Admiralty's search for a seagoing fighter able to hold its own in combat, and two specifications of 1938 were chewed over for two years and then amalgamated in 1940. By this time the talking had to lead somewhere, and it is to the credit of Fairey Aviation that the resulting Firefly Mk I was in the air before the end of 1941. This was essentially a tremendously improved Fulmar, with a Griffon engine, patented Youngman high-lift flaps, the fashionable elliptical wing and four cannon. Good features included excellent handling at low speeds and a pilot view better than for any other tailwheel type fighter, the pilot having a bulged canopy above the leading edge. The Firefly F.I could also carry up to 2,000 lb (907 kg) of bombs or eight 60-lb (27-kg) rockets, and towards the end of the war flew effective ground-attack missions. Drawbacks were that Fairey's chaotic administration delayed release in numbers until late 1943, and the basic fact that a large two-seater simply could not have the same performance as other fighters. Like the

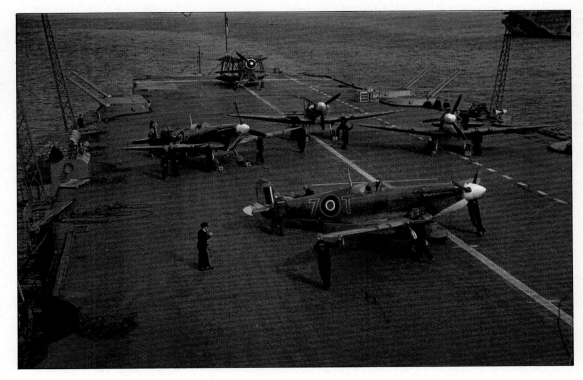

Seafire IIC trainers being manhandled on the deck of a Royal Navy fleet carrier (note the folded Albacore at the stern). This mark did not have folding wings, and retained the Rotol three-blade propeller of many Spitfire Vs.

The CAM (Catapult-Armed Merchantman) ships were not exactly aircraft carriers, but they could fire Hurricane or Sea Hurricane fighters with the aid of cordite rockets. After engaging the enemy the luckless fighter pilot then had to take to his parachute — perhaps into the North Atlantic in winter, lethal in about a minute's exposure — and be picked up by a friendly vessel.

Fulmar the Firefly had no defence to the rear, and in combat had to rely on its good turn radius with the flaps in the high-lift mode, and the skill of the pilot. From the 471st Firefly a more powerful engine was fitted, and production included the FR.1 with ASH radar for detecting hostile ships and U-boats, the NF.2 night fighter with A1 Mk X radar and, at the end of the war, the much more powerful FR.4 with a two-stage Griffon and radiators moved to the leading edge.

There were numerous naval fighters that never reached the wartime squadrons. One of Blackburn's designs, the B-44 to specification N.2/42, was for a Sabre-engined seaplane with a float retracting in the air to form the underside of the fuselage (rather like a variable-height flying-boat). This was dropped, but the same company spent the entire war trying to develop a single-seat fighter able to carry a torpedo. Such a machine could never have been a good fighter — except for shooting down aircraft other than fighters — but in aiming torpedoes against

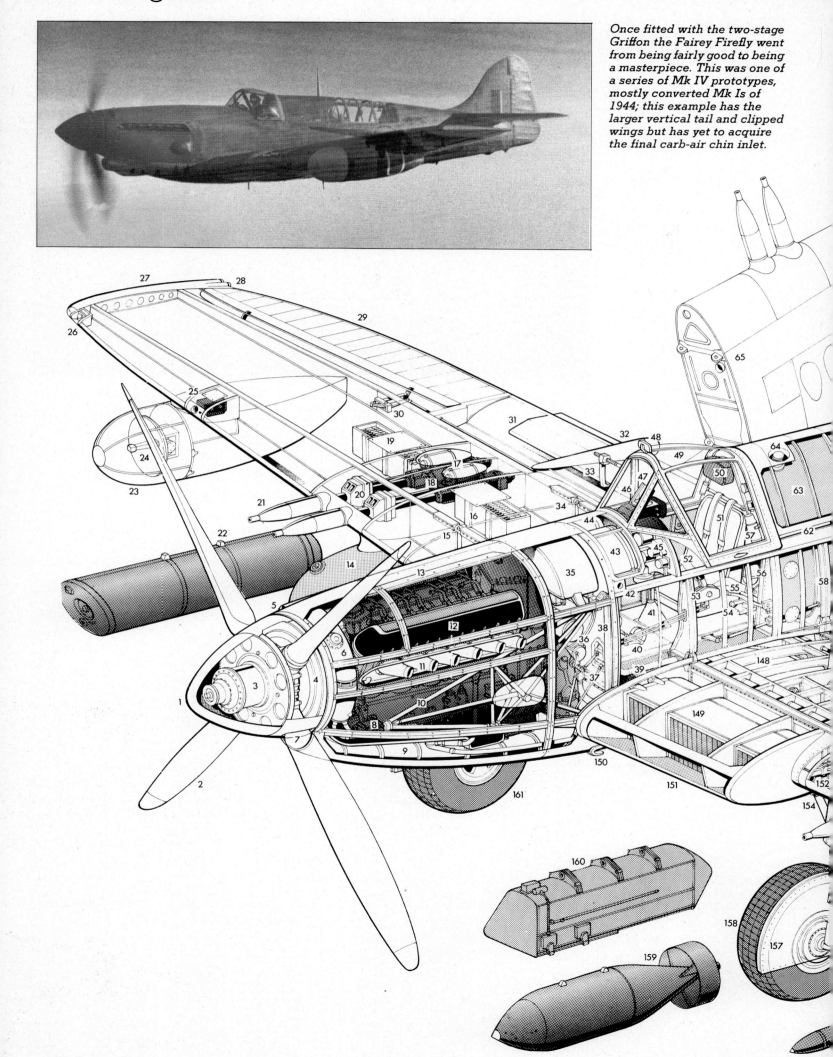

Once fitted with the two-stage Griffon the Fairey Firefly went from being fairly good to being a masterpiece. This was one of a series of Mk IV prototypes, mostly converted Mk Is of 1944; this example has the larger vertical tail and clipped wings but has yet to acquire the final carb-air chin inlet.

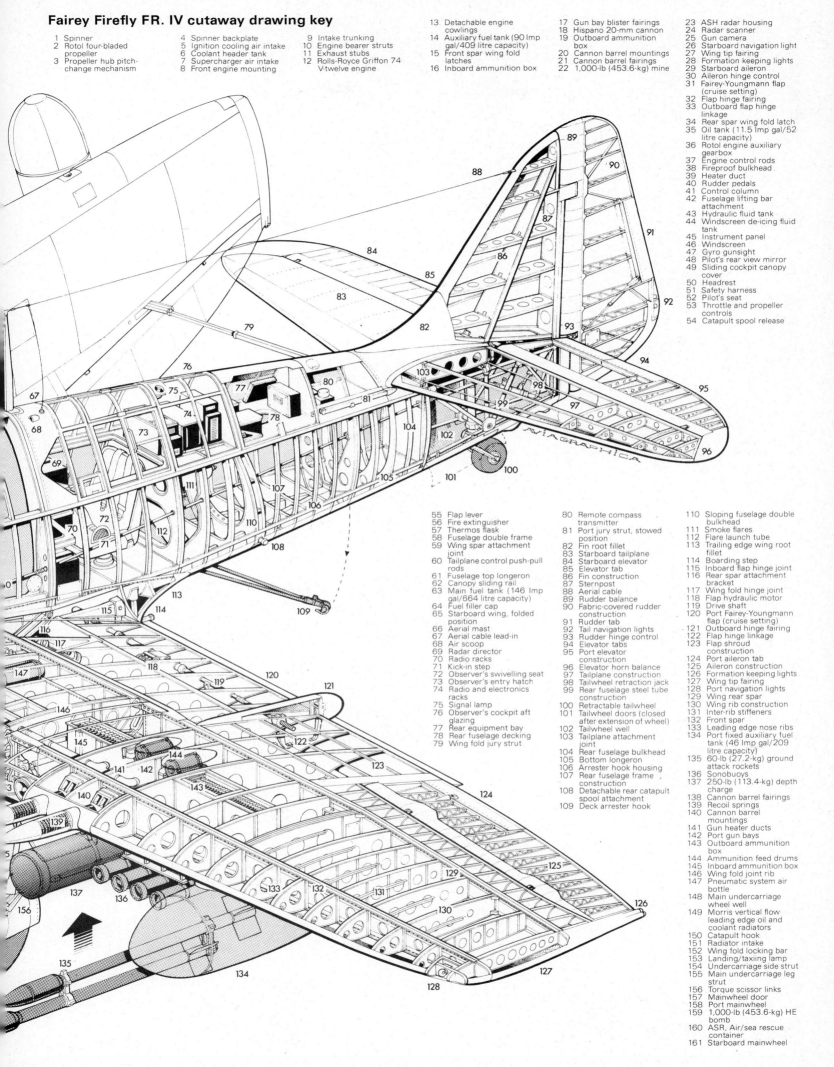

Fairey Firefly FR. IV cutaway drawing key

1 Spinner
2 Rotol four-bladed propeller
3 Propeller hub pitch-change mechanism
4 Spinner backplate
5 Ignition cooling air intake
6 Coolant header tank
7 Supercharger air intake
8 Front engine mounting
9 Intake trunking
10 Engine bearer struts
11 Exhaust stubs
12 Rolls-Royce Griffon 74 V-twelve engine
13 Detachable engine cowlings
14 Auxiliary fuel tank (90 Imp gal/409 litre capacity)
15 Front spar wing fold latches
16 Inboard ammunition box
17 Gun bay blister fairings
18 Hispano 20-mm cannon
19 Outboard ammunition box
20 Cannon barrel mountings
21 Cannon barrel fairings
22 1,000-lb (453.6-kg) mine
23 ASH radar housing
24 Radar scanner
25 Gun camera
26 Starboard navigation light
27 Wing tip fairing
28 Formation keeping lights
29 Starboard aileron
30 Aileron hinge control
31 Fairey-Youngmann flap (cruise setting)
32 Flap hinge fairing
33 Outboard flap hinge linkage
34 Rear spar wing fold latch
35 Oil tank (11.5 Imp gal/52 litre capacity)
36 Rotol engine auxiliary gearbox
37 Engine control rods
38 Fireproof bulkhead
39 Heater duct
40 Rudder pedals
41 Control column
42 Fuselage lifting bar attachment
43 Hydraulic fluid tank
44 Windscreen de-icing fluid tank
45 Instrument panel
46 Windscreen
47 Gyro gunsight
48 Pilot's rear view mirror
49 Sliding cockpit canopy cover
50 Headrest
51 Safety harness
52 Pilot's seat
53 Throttle and propeller controls
54 Catapult spool release

55 Flap lever
56 Fire extinguisher
57 Thermos flask
58 Fuselage double frame
59 Wing spar attachment joint
60 Tailplane control push-pull rods
61 Fuselage top longeron
62 Canopy sliding rail
63 Main fuel tank (146 Imp gal/664 litre capacity)
64 Fuel filler cap
65 Starboard wing, folded position
66 Aerial mast
67 Aerial cable lead-in
68 Air scoop
69 Radar director
70 Radio racks
71 Kick-in step
72 Observer's swivelling seat
73 Observer's entry hatch
74 Radio and electronics racks
75 Signal lamp
76 Observer's cockpit aft glazing
77 Rear equipment bay
78 Rear fuselage decking
79 Wing fold jury strut
80 Remote compass transmitter
81 Port jury strut, stowed position
82 Fin root fillet
83 Starboard tailplane
84 Starboard elevator
85 Elevator tab
86 Fin construction
87 Sternpost
88 Aerial cable
89 Rudder balance
90 Fabric-covered rudder construction
91 Rudder tab
92 Tail navigation lights
93 Rudder hinge control
94 Elevator tabs
95 Port elevator construction
96 Elevator horn balance
97 Tailplane construction
98 Tailwheel retraction jack
99 Rear fuselage steel tube construction
100 Retractable tailwheel
101 Tailwheel doors (closed after extension of wheel)
102 Tailwheel well
103 Tailplane attachment joint
104 Rear fuselage bulkhead
105 Bottom longeron
106 Arrester hook housing
107 Rear fuselage frame construction
108 Detachable rear catapult spool attachment
109 Deck arrester hook
110 Sloping fuselage double bulkhead
111 Smoke flares
112 Flare launch tube
113 Trailing edge wing root fillet
114 Boarding step
115 Inboard flap hinge joint
116 Rear spar attachment bracket
117 Wing fold hinge joint
118 Flap hydraulic motor
119 Drive shaft
120 Port Fairey-Youngmann flap (cruise setting)
121 Outboard hinge fairing
122 Flap hinge linkage
123 Flap shroud construction
124 Port aileron tab
125 Aileron construction
126 Formation keeping lights
127 Wing tip fairing
128 Port navigation lights
129 Wing rear spar
130 Wing rib construction
131 Inter-rib stiffeners
132 Front spar
133 Leading edge nose ribs
134 Port fixed auxiliary fuel tank (46 Imp gal/209 litre capacity)
135 60-lb (27.2-kg) ground attack rockets
136 Sonobuoys
137 250-lb (113.4-kg) depth charge
138 Cannon barrel fairings
139 Recoil springs
140 Cannon barrel mountings
141 Gun heater ducts
142 Port gun bays
143 Outboard ammunition box
144 Ammunition feed drums
145 Inboard ammunition box
146 Wing fold joint rib
147 Pneumatic system air bottle
148 Main undercarriage wheel well
149 Morris vertical flow leading edge oil and coolant radiators
150 Catapult hook
151 Radiator intake
152 Wing fold locking bar
153 Landing/taxiing lamp
154 Undercarriage side strut
155 Main undercarriage leg strut
156 Torque scissor links
157 Mainwheel door
158 Port mainwheel
159 1,000-lb (453.6-kg) HE bomb
160 ASR, Air/sea rescue container
161 Starboard mainwheel

Naval Fighters

Though burdened by a navigator (observer) and much deadweight called for by naval use, the Firefly I and other wartime marks had just enough performance to be useful, though they were outclassed in combat with Japanese single-seaters. This F.I served aboard HMS Indefatigable.

Possibly taken on the last day of the war, this photograph shows Lt-Cdr E.M. 'Winkle' Brown making deck trials with the first Hawker Sea Fury aboard the light carrier HMS Formidable. This aircraft was a staggering contrast compared with the wartime British naval fighters.

The worst thing about the Firebrand was the seven years it took to develop, so that only six Sabre-engined Mk IIs reached the Navy (non-operational, with No. 708 Sqn) during the war. This photograph shows the version that finally made the grade, the Centaurus-powered TF.IV, seen on test in July 1945.

Though only peripherally fighters, the Sea Mosquito TR.33s had four cannon and could give as good an account of themselves at low level as any other fighter Mosquito. These multi-role aircraft could carry a torpedo, and their radar was primarily for use against surface targets.

warships it would have been slightly less vulnerable than the 104 mph (167 km/h) Swordfish. Named Firebrand, the first of these versatile machines flew in February 1942. Most wartime Firebrands had the troublesome Sabre engine, but the version which at last went into production had the air-cooled Centaurus, and the TF.4 (torpedo fighter) version at last entered service in September 1945, a month after the fighting stopped.

At the end of the war Hawker was well advanced with the Sea Fury Mk X, first flown in February 1945 as the carrier version of what had begun as the Tempest Light Fighter. This outstanding Centaurus-powered machine later became the FAA's last piston-engine fighter-bomber and saw action in Korea. Westland took on the difficult job of making a successor to the Firebrand and eventually, years after the war, the Wyvern entered service powered by the Python turboprop.

Night and Long-range Fighters

Until late in the Battle of Britain the only long-range or night fighter in the RAF was a poorly armed converted bomber. The massive Beaufighter and brilliant Mosquito then at last rectified the gaps left by the official procurement machine.

The most numerous mark of Mosquito was the FB.VI fighter-bomber, which combined the guns of the Mk II with a substantial bomb or rocket load.

In the simple days before World War II a night-fighter was just a day fighter with night equipment, such as a battery, navigation lights, cockpit lighting and flares which could be dropped to illuminate the landing field. The actual task of finding enemy aircraft at night was so difficult it was largely ignored; there were no set rules or techniques and, as far as the UK was concerned, not even an effective defence organisation such as had been created 'the hard way' in World War I.

Salvation lay in the invention of radar. Though the UK was not — as is often supposed — the only country to develop radar before World War II, British workers did achieve one tremendous advance that transformed the possibility of fitting radar into an aircraft. This was the magnetron valve, the creator of microwaves as now found in millions of factories and kitchens to generate radio waves with a wavelength of a few centimetres. Such short waves matched radars that could go into vehicles, including aircraft, and so transformed the war, tilting the balance for a while (until magnetrons were captured by the enemy) in favour of the Allies. But a handful of brilliant engineers, led by Dr Ted Bowen, created airborne radar (at the time called RDF.2) even before the magnetron existed.

British Fighters of World War II

This Blenheim, originally built in 1936 as one of the first Mk I bombers, was converted to IF fighter standard in late 1938 and then fitted with AI Mk II radar in late 1939. It is shown after withdrawal from front-line duty, serving with No. 54 OTU (Operational Training Unit) at Church Fenton in 1941.

Potentially very important night fighters, the various sub-types of Douglas Havoc were mainly frittered away on LAM (aerial mine) and Turbinlite (aerial searchlight) trials. This example was an early Twin Wasp-powered Havoc I three-seat intruder, of No. 23 Sqn at Ford.

The Mosquito II night-fighter brought a great increase in flight performance, and with the original AI Mk IV radar it was possible to mount four machine-guns in the nose as well as four 20-mm cannon under the cockpit floor.

A transmitter capable of fitting an aeroplane yet working on wavelengths of several metres (7 m was chosen in January 1937) could not have much power. The peak power of the pulses of the first set was 95 watts, about the same as an electric-light bulb, and the set first flew in an Anson on 16 August 1937. After intensive development this led to a fully engineered set called AI (Airborne Interception) Mk I, flown in a Fairey Battle on 21 May 1939. Though it was temperamental, could lie convincingly and went wrong at the drop of a hat, it could occasionally indicate the presence, and rough direction and range, of a hostile aircraft from a distance about the same as the set's height above the ground (up to about 20,000 ft/6095 m, or 3.8 miles/6.1 km). But the task of finding a target among the dim flickering 'grass' on the cathode-ray tubes called for great skill by the operator. In early sets there was one display to give an up/down indication and a second to give left/right, both giving an idea of target range.

A priceless colour photograph taken by Charles E. Brown showing the Hurricane IIC night intruder flown by the CO of No. 87 Sqn in 1941-2. Though not equal to the German single-seaters, the Hurricane proved valuable as a night fighter, attack bomber, naval fighter, rocket carrier and big-gun tank buster.

This Defiant is so weatherbeaten that it is difficult to read the code letters. DZ identified the famed No. 151 Sqn, but PZ (Australian No. 456 Sqn) also adorned Defiants in late 1941.

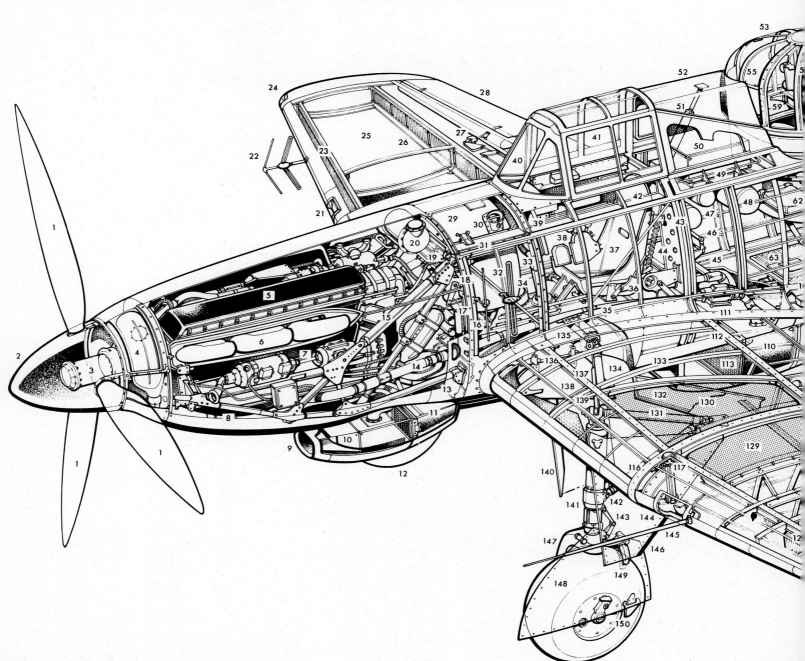

Boulton Paul Defiant II cutaway drawing key

1 Three-bladed Rotol propeller, diameter 11 ft 9 in (3.58 m)
2 Spinner
3 Propeller hub
4 Coolant header tank
5 Rolls-Royce Merlin XX 12-cyl Vee engine
6 Exhaust manifold
7 Engine accessories
8 Engine bearer support
9 Oil cooler intake
10 Intake duct
11 Oil cooler fairing
12 Starboard mainwheel
13 Engine bearer/bulkhead lower attachment
14 Coolant pipe
15 Engine bearer
16 Oil filter
17 Engine control linkage
18 Forward firewall/bulkhead
19 Engine bearer/bulkhead upper attachment
20 Hydraulic reservoir
21 Starboard landing lamp
22 AI Mk VI radar transmitter aerial
23 Wing front spar
24 Starboard navigation light
25 Wing undersurface (load-bearing)
26 Wing rear spar
27 Aileron control linkage
28 Starboard aileron
29 Oil tank, capacity 10 Imp gal (45 litres)
30 Oil tank filler cap
31 Tank attachment
32 AI Mk VI receiver (azimuth) aerials
33 Control column
34 Compass
35 Wingroot fairing
36 Seat support frame
37 Pilot's seat
38 Throttle quadrant
39 Instrument panel
40 Windscreen
41 Cockpit canopy
42 Cockpit coaming
43 Fuselage/rear spar frame (No. 7)
44 Seat adjustment
45 Aileron control linkage assembly (accumulator and power unit frame deleted for clarity)
46 Pilot's safety harness attachment
47 Compressed air cylinder (brakes/dorsal fairings)
48 De-icing tank
49 W/T crate mounting frame
50 Transmitter/receiver, TR.113A or TR.9D
51 Fairing actuating ram

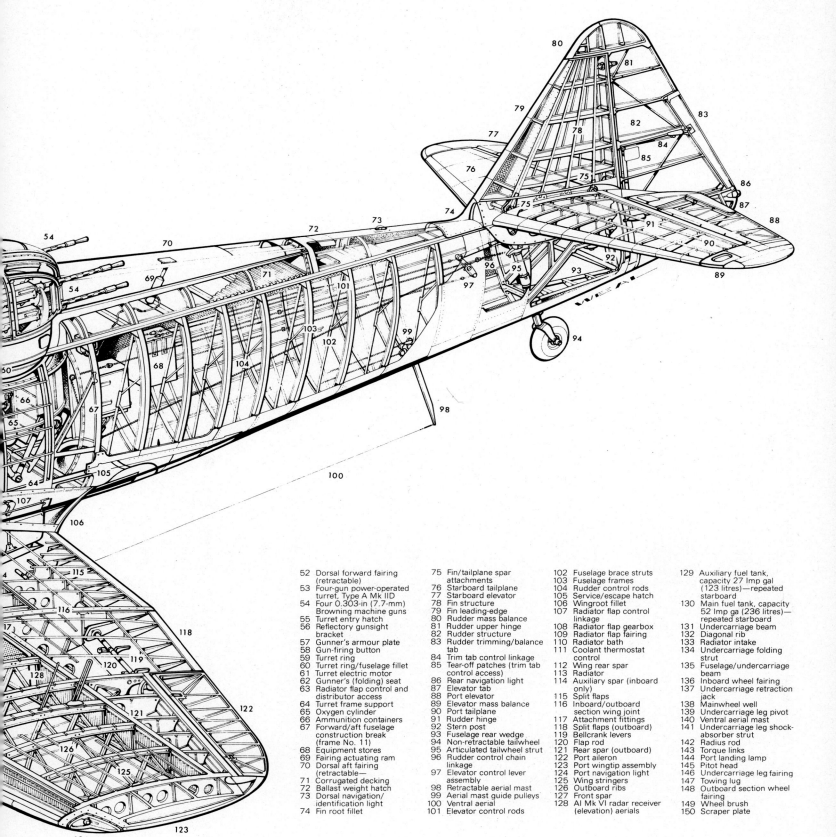

52 Dorsal forward fairing (retractable)
53 Four-gun power-operated turret, Type A Mk IID
54 Four 0.303-in (7.7-mm) Browning machine guns
55 Turret entry hatch
56 Reflectory gunsight bracket
57 Gunner's armour plate
58 Gun-firing button
59 Turret ring
60 Turret ring/fuselage fillet
61 Turret electric motor
62 Gunner's (folding) seat
63 Radiator flap control and distributor access
64 Turret frame support
65 Oxygen cylinder
66 Ammunition containers
67 Forward/aft fuselage construction break (frame No. 11)
68 Equipment stores
69 Fairing actuating ram
70 Dorsal aft fairing (retractable—
71 Corrugated decking
72 Ballast weight hatch
73 Dorsal navigation/identification light
74 Fin root fillet
75 Fin/tailplane spar attachments
76 Starboard tailplane
77 Starboard elevator
78 Fin structure
79 Fin leading-edge
80 Rudder mass balance
81 Rudder upper hinge
82 Rudder structure
83 Rudder trimming/balance tab
84 Trim tab control linkage
85 Tear-off patches (trim tab control access)
86 Rear navigation light
87 Elevator tab
88 Port elevator
89 Elevator mass balance
90 Port tailplane
91 Rudder hinge
92 Stern post
93 Fuselage rear wedge
94 Non-retractable tailwheel
95 Articulated tailwheel strut
96 Rudder control chain linkage
97 Elevator control lever assembly
98 Retractable aerial mast
99 Aerial mast guide pulleys
100 Ventral aerial
101 Elevator control rods
102 Fuselage brace struts
103 Fuselage frames
104 Rudder control rods
105 Service/escape hatch
106 Wingroot fillet
107 Radiator flap control linkage
108 Radiator flap gearbox
109 Radiator flap fairing
110 Radiator bath
111 Coolant thermostat control
112 Wing rear spar
113 Radiator
114 Auxiliary spar (inboard only)
115 Split flaps
116 Inboard/outboard section wing joint
117 Attachment fittings
118 Split flaps (outboard)
119 Bellcrank levers
120 Flap rod
121 Rear spar (outboard)
122 Port aileron
123 Port wingtip assembly
124 Port navigation light
125 Wing stringers
126 Outboard ribs
127 Front spar
128 AI Mk VI radar receiver (elevation) aerials
129 Auxiliary fuel tank, capacity 27 Imp gal (123 litres)—repeated starboard
130 Main fuel tank, capacity 52 Imp ga (236 litres)—repeated starboard
131 Undercarriage beam
132 Diagonal rib
133 Radiator intake
134 Undercarriage folding strut
135 Fuselage/undercarriage beam
136 Inboard wheel fairing
137 Undercarriage retraction jack
138 Mainwheel well
139 Undercarriage leg pivot
140 Ventral aerial mast
141 Undercarriage leg shock-absorber strut
142 Radius rod
143 Torque links
144 Port landing lamp
145 Pitot head
146 Undercarriage leg fairing
147 Towing lug
148 Outboard section wheel fairing
149 Wheel brush
150 Scraper plate

Boulton Paul Defiant

SPECIFICATION

Type: two-seat night fighter
Powerplant: (Mk II) one 1,280-hp (954-kW) Rolls-Royce Merlin XX V-12 piston engine
Performance: maximum speed 313 mph (504 km/h) at 19,000 ft (5790 m); cruising speed 260 mph (418 km/h); service ceiling 30,350 ft (9250 m); range 465 miles (748 km)
Weights: empty 6,282 lb (2849 kg); maximum take-off 8,424 lb (3821 kg)
Dimensions: span 39 ft 4 in (11.99 m); length 35 ft 4 in (10.77 m); height 11 ft 4 in (3.45 m); wing area 250 sq ft (23.23 m²)
Armament: four 0.303-in (7.7-mm) machine guns in power-operated dorsal turret

Defiant NF.II with AI Mk VI radar, of No. 151 Sqn

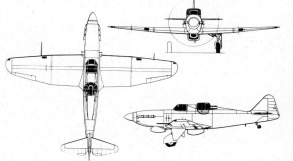

Boulton Paul Defiant NF.II

Defiant NF.II with A1. VI radar

Defiants of No. 264 Sqn, the original user of this turret-armed fighter in daylight in early 1940. The photograph was taken during the Blitz period, before these aircraft had radar (and when B-type roundels were used with abnormally wide yellow outer rings).

The first radar-equipped night fighters were 21 Blenheim Mk IFs, hastily fitted with AI Mk II in July/September 1939. In the first half of 1940 over 60 Blenheims received the somewhat better AI Mk III. Most aircrew disliked and resisted the new invention (it was even worse in the Luftwaffe where officer pilots refused to accept steering commands from sergeants sitting in the back), and many officials campaigned to have AI radar abandoned. The officials could not understand radar, but they could comprehend such crazy ideas as the Turbinlite and LAM. The former was a searchlight, carried in a large aircraft. In fact, to know where to aim the light the carrier had to have AI radar; and instead of projecting a beam of light it would have been better to have projected cannon shells. Instead the idea was that, once the hostile aircraft was nicely illuminated, and staying straight and level so that the searchlight stayed on target, Hurricanes could come in and shoot it down. Officials must have been puzzled that years of effort by large numbers of aircraft on

Portugal received Beaufighters during the war, and this ex-RAF TF.X torpedo-fighter served with No. 8 Sqn at Portela de Sacavem in 1945-50.

In the Mediterranean theatre most Beaufighters were used for long-range day escort and ground attack, this Fairey-built Mk IC of RAF No. 252 Sqn having been modified with the dihedral tailplane in early 1942. This was one of several colour schemes used in that theatre (in this case in Egypt).

this crazy scheme succeeded in shooting down only one aircraft, and that belonged to the RAF. The main Turbinlite carrier was the excellent Douglas Havoc, a British conversion of an American light bomber with outstanding performance, but some Bristol Beaufighter and de Havilland Mosquito conversions were also made.

Limited successes

LAM stood for Long Aerial Mine, and it was a natural step from LAM (said as a word) to its code name of 'Mutton'. Again the main night fighter involved was the Havoc, and the idea was to suspend a small bomb on a 2,000-ft (610-m) cable, either towed behind the fighter or allowed to fall on a parachute. An aircraft flying into the cable was expected to draw the bomb smartly up against itself, to explode on impact. This again appealed to technology illiterates, and the whole of 1941-2 was wasted on a technique that was quite dangerous — to its exponents.

But if these harebrained schemes brought little success, neither at first did AI radar. The technical difficulties, combined with the total disbelief of its operators, told against it in 1940-1, and the few night victories were gained by black-painted Hurricanes, Spitfires, Blenheims and Defiants, carrying little special equipment beyond metal plates to shield the exhaust from the pilot's eyes. In late August 1940 the RAF received another of its great warplanes that resulted from initiative by the manufacturer. The Bristol Beaufighter was created quickly by fitting two

Hurricane I night fighters depart at dusk, probably in late 1940. Though not equipped with radar, the Hurricane had one of the best success rates of all RAF fighters at night in the pre-1942 era.

Bristol Beaufighter

SPECIFICATION

Type: two-seat night/long-range/anti-shipping strike fighter

Powerplant: (TF.Mk X) two 1,770-hp (1320-kW) Bristol Hercules XVIII radial piston engines

Performance: maximum speed 303 mph (488 km/h) at 1,300 ft (395 m); maximum cruising speed 249 mph (401 km/h) at 5,000 ft (1525 m); service ceiling 15,000 ft (4570 m); range 1,470 miles (2366 km)

Weights: empty 15,600 lb (7076 kg); maximum take-off 25,200 lb (11431 kg)

Dimensions: span 57 ft 10 in (17.63 m); length 41 ft 8 in (12.70 m); height 15 ft 10 in (4.83 m); wing area 503 sq ft (46.73 m²)

Armament: four forward-firing

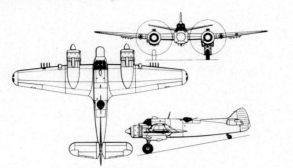

Bristol Beaufighter Mk I, No. 25 Sqn at North Weald, September 1940.

20-mm cannon, six forward-firing 0.303-in (7.7-mm) machine-guns and one 0.303-in (7.7-mm) Vickers 'K' gun in dorsal position, plus one torpedo, and two 250-lb (113-kg) bombs or eight 90-lb (41-kg) rocket projectiles

Bristol Beaufighter TF.X

Operations in the Mediterranean theatre quickly caused aircraft to deteriorate, and this Beaufighter IC looks war-weary. Still with the horizontal tailplane, with which swing on take-off and longitudinal instability at low speeds caused severe problems, this aircraft was probably operating in Tunisia in early 1943.

Though in no way inferior to other variants as a day fighter, the Beaufighter IC was intended for Coastal Command or desert missions chiefly against surface targets. The nearer aircraft has a non-dihedral tailplane; the observer can be seen facing forward, while the DF loop fairing above the fuselage is prominent on both aircraft.

powerful Hercules engines on the wing of a Beaufort torpedo bomber, and fitting a new fuselage with a pilot in the nose, an observer at the back and four cannon under the floor. For good measure six machine-guns were added in the wings, and the 'Beau' was also tailor-made to carry radar. It joined the RAF without it, but by November 1940 the first Beaufighter Mk IFs were in service with the new AI Mk IV radar. Like the Mk III this sent out its pulses of radio waves from a nose aerial looking like a harpoon, and received echoes on vertical or inclined dipoles on the outer wings, so connected up that they furnished the operator with the azimuth and elevation (direction in the horizontal and vertical planes) of the target.

Deadly at night

In the Beaufighter the observer sat far removed from the pilot, under a transparent cupola, his swivelling sear usually facing aft so that he could attend to the radar displays and controls. Between passing steering commands to the pilot he had to change the drums of ammunition on

An invasion-striped Beaufighter VI of No. 445 Sqn, RAAF, operating with a Coastal Command strike wing in 1944, salvoes rockets whilst in level flight against simulated targets.

Night and Long-range Fighters

The world's first aircraft radomes were constructed in autumn 1941 to cover the scanner of AI Mk VII, the first centimetric radar, which first flew in November 1941 in Beaufighter IF X7579. Soon called a 'thimble' radome, it had no effect on flying qualities.

The heroic defence of Malta from the summer of 1940 had been sharply reduced by a lack of night-fighters. When Beaufighters were received in 1941 they lacked radar, but still operated round the clock. This Mk IF taxiing at Luqa is probably from the initial detachment of No. 89 Sqn.

the four cannon, until at the 401st aircraft this arrangement was changed for the belt feed that Bristol had recommended from the very start. In daylight the Beaufighter was at a disadvantage in close combat with a smaller fighter, but at night it was deadly, once the total night system of ground radar, ground controller, secure radio voice communications, reliable airborne radar and a good team of observer and pilot had been put together.

By 1941 an even better night-fighter was flying, again the result of company initiative triumphing over hordes of officials who tried to kill the idea. The aircraft was the Mosquito, and after being delayed for a year before the war was at last allowed to go ahead in a batch of 50. Lord Beaverbrook, appointed Minister of Aircraft Production after Dunkirk, had no time for so small a programme and tried to cancel it, but once the prototype had flown in November 1940 this wooden twin-Merlin aircraft was uncancellable. It was simply too good, and could outfly a

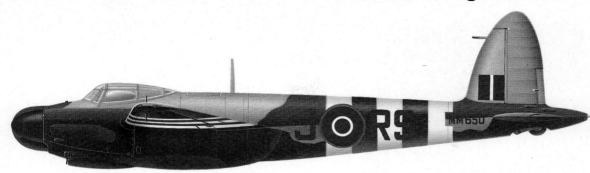

MM650 was a Mosquito NF.XIX, one of the best of the wartime night fighters with a so-called 'bull nose' which in this aircraft housed the American SCR-720 radar (AI Mk X). It is shown in invasion stripes operating from Swannington with No. 157 Sqn, with two-stage Merlins.

This Mosquito FB.6 (post-war designation) was built in 1945 by Airspeed and is shown in post-war markings while operating from Wahn (Cologne) and Celle with the British Air Force of Occupation. The badge of the unit, No. 4 Sqn, appears on the fin.

Hurricane with one engine feathered. Of the batch of 50, 30 were to be fighters, with four cannon under the nose, four machine-guns in the nose, a door on the right side to the side-by-side cockpit, a wide flat bullet proof windscreen and the AI Mk IV radar. Faster than a 1941 Spitfire, this fine aircraft was later developed in many other night-fighter versions.

The magnetron valve led the way to radar working on centimetric wavelengths, and the resulting AI Mk VIII first flew in a Beaufighter in November 1941. Instead of spidery aerials it had a new shape, a so-called thimble nose radome, and the new radar had important advantages in projecting a pencil-like beam ahead of the fighter. The beam could be scanned (pointed) in various repeating patterns, and give clearer pictures of the enemy's position, especially at low level where the previous sets were almost useless. By March 1943 the speedier Mosquito had appeared in Mk XII form with a thimble nose radar, which necessitated removal of the four

This Mosquito FB.VI was almost certainly home-based with Coastal Command. The rockets being loaded have the slender 25-lb (11-kg) armour-piercing heads, though for soft-skinned ships the 60-lb (27-kg) high-explosive pattern was also used.

T4638

Bristol Beaufighter

T4638 was the 16th Beaufighter IF produced by Fairey Aviation at Stockport. It was fitted with AI Mk IV radar before delivery to No. 604 (County of Middlesex) Sqn, AAF, in 1941, serving alongside the Merlin-engined Beaufighter II. Attrition was severe, entirely because of the basic difficulty of flying by night. Note the long flame-damping exhaust pipes.

Night and Long-range Fighters

The last wartime Beaufighter mark, in which all deficiencies were rectified, was the Mk X (called Mk 10 post-war). This had a different mark of Hercules engine, a Mk VIII radar used mainly in the surface attack mode, larger elevators and, in later examples, a dorsal fin. Full gun armament was retained, plus ability to carry a torpedo or, as in this aircraft of No. 445 Sqn, RAAF, eight rockets. The observer had a Vickers 'K' for rear defence.

Bristol Beaufighter I cutaway drawing key

1 Starboard navigation light (fore) and formation-keeping light (aft)
2 Wing structure
3 Aileron adjustable tab
4 Starboard aileron
5 Four Browning 0.303-in (7.7-mm) machine guns
6 Machine gun ports
7 Starboard outer wing fuel tank, capacity 87 Imp gal (395 litres)
8 Split trailing-edge flaps, hydraulically actuated
9 Starboard flap
10 Flap operating jack
11 Starboard nacelle tail fairing
12 Oil tank, capacity 17 Imp gal (77 litres)
13 Starboard inner wing fuel tank, capacity 188 Imp gal (855 litres)
14 Cabin air duct
15 Hinged leading-edge sections
16 Engine bulkhead
17 Engine bearers
18 Auxiliary intake
19 Supercharger air intake
20 Engine cooling flaps
21 1,650 hp Bristol Hercules III radial engine
22 De Havilland Hydromatic airscrew
23 Airscrew spinner
24 Lockheed oleo-pneumatic shock-absorber
25 Starboard mainwheel, with Dunlop brakes
26 Forward identification lamp in nose cap
27 Rudder pedals
28 Control column
29 Cannon ports
30 Seat adjusting lever
31 Pilot's seat
32 Instrument panel
33 Clear-vision panel
34 Flat bullet proof windscreen
35 Fixed canopy (sideways-hinged on later aircraft)
36 Spar carry-through step
37 Nose centre section attachment point
38 Fuselage/centre section attachment point
39 Pilot's entry/emergency escape hatchway
40 Underfloor cannon blast tubes
41 Fuselage/centre section attachment points

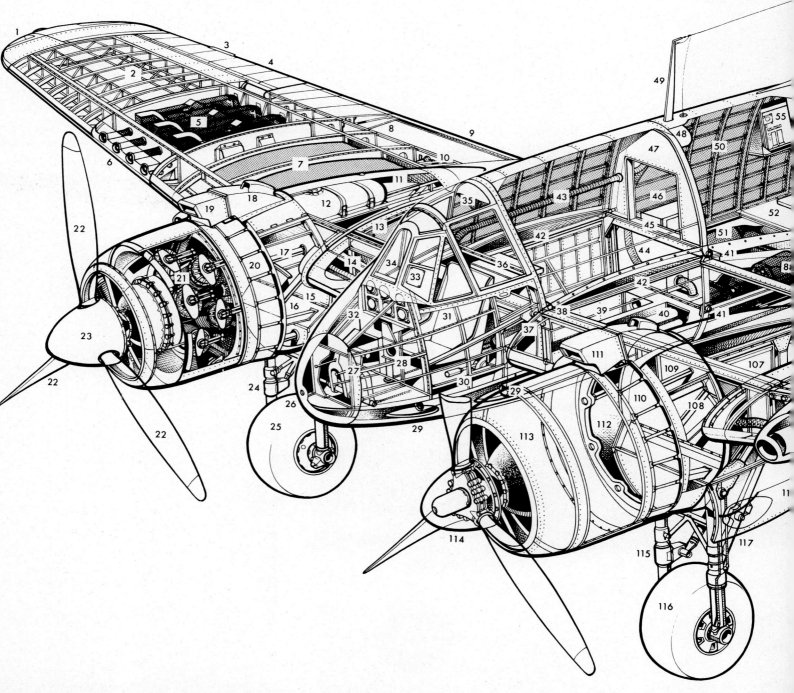

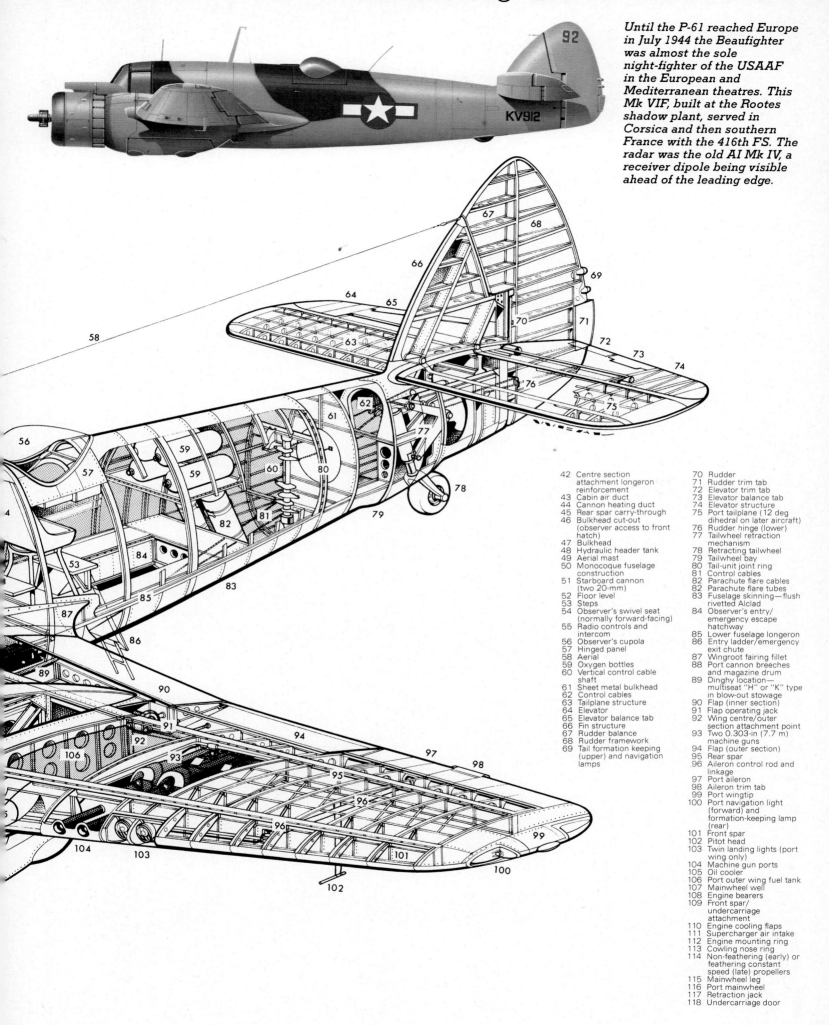

Until the P-61 reached Europe in July 1944 the Beaufighter was almost the sole night-fighter of the USAAF in the European and Mediterranean theatres. This Mk VIF, built at the Rootes shadow plant, served in Corsica and then southern France with the 416th FS. The radar was the old AI Mk IV, a receiver dipole being visible ahead of the leading edge.

42 Centre section attachment longeron reinforcement
43 Cabin air duct
44 Cannon heating duct
45 Rear spar carry-through
46 Bulkhead cut-out (observer access to front hatch)
47 Bulkhead
48 Hydraulic header tank
49 Aerial mast
50 Monocoque fuselage construction
51 Starboard cannon (two 20-mm)
52 Floor level
53 Steps
54 Observer's swivel seat (normally forward-facing)
55 Radio controls and intercom
56 Observer's cupola
57 Hinged panel
58 Aerial
59 Oxygen bottles
60 Vertical control cable shaft
61 Sheet metal bulkhead
62 Control cables
63 Tailplane structure
64 Elevator
65 Elevator balance tab
66 Fin structure
67 Rudder balance
68 Rudder framework
69 Tail formation keeping (upper) and navigation lamps
70 Rudder
71 Rudder trim tab
72 Elevator trim tab
73 Elevator balance tab
74 Elevator structure
75 Port tailplane (12 deg dihedral on later aircraft)
76 Rudder hinge (lower)
77 Tailwheel retraction mechanism
78 Retracting tailwheel
79 Tailwheel bay
80 Tail-unit joint ring
81 Control cables
82 Parachute flare cables
82 Parachute flare tubes
83 Fuselage skinning—flush rivetted Alclad
84 Observer's entry/emergency escape hatchway
85 Lower fuselage longeron
86 Entry ladder/emergency exit chute
87 Wingroot fairing fillet
88 Port cannon breeches and magazine drum
89 Dinghy location—multiseat "H" or "K" type in blow-out stowage
90 Flap (inner section)
91 Flap operating jack
92 Wing centre/outer section attachment point
93 Two 0.303-in (7.7 m) machine guns
94 Flap (outer section)
95 Rear spar
96 Aileron control rod and linkage
97 Port aileron
98 Aileron trim tab
99 Port wingtip
100 Port navigation light (forward) and formation-keeping lamp (rear)
101 Front spar
102 Pitot head
103 Twin landing lights (port wing only)
104 Machine gun ports
105 Oil cooler
106 Port outer wing fuel tank
107 Mainwheel well
108 Engine bearers
109 Front spar/undercarriage attachment
110 Engine cooling flaps
111 Supercharger air intake
112 Engine mounting ring
113 Cowling nose ring
114 Non-feathering (early) or feathering constant speed (late) propellers
115 Mainwheel leg
116 Port mainwheel
117 Retraction jack
118 Undercarriage door

de Havilland Mosquito

SPECIFICATION

Type: two-seat bomber, fighter-bomber, night fighter and photographic reconnaissance aircraft

Powerplant: (FB.Mk VI) two 1.620-hp (1208-kW) Rolls-Royce Merlin 25 V-12 piston engines

Performance: maximum speed 362 mph (583 km/h) at 5,500 ft (167 m); maximum cruising speed 325 mph (523 km/h) at 15,000 ft (4570 m); service ceiling 33,000 ft (10060 m); range with internal bomb load 1,650 miles (2655 km)

Weights: empty 14,300 lb (6486 kg); maximum take-off weight 22,300 lb (10115 kg) (1675 m); maximum cruising

Dimensions: span 54 ft 2 in (16.51 m); length 40 ft 10¾ in (12.47 m); height 15 ft 3 in (4.65 m); wing area 454 sq ft (42.18 m²)

Armament: four 20-mm cannon and four 0.303-in (7.7-mm) machine-guns in nose, plus 2,000 lb (907 kg) of bombs, or 1,000 lb (454 kg) of bombs and eight 60-lb (27-kg) rocket projectiles

Mosquito FB.VI fighter-bomber built by Standard Motors at Canley (Coventry), one of a batch of 38 sent to Australia and renumbered with RAAF serial.

de Havilland Mosquito Mk IV Series 2

Mosquitoes first operated from bases outside Britain from December 1942 when No. 23 Sqn took its Mk II night-fighters to Luqa, Malta. They quickly scored by night and day against aircraft and ground targets. This aircraft has no radar, though it was retained by at least some of No. 23's aircraft.

machine-guns. Marshall's at Cambridge quickly converted 97 Mosquito F.IIs to NF.XII standard with a bull nose radome over AI Mk VIII, and these entered service at Hunsdon in late March 1943 with No.85 Sqn, commanded by the RAF's most famous night-fighter pilot, John Cunningham (like Beamont, after the war a famous test pilot). These were followed by 270 NF.XIIIs with the improved airframe of the Mosquito FB.VI and increased fuel capacity. Then Marshall's converted Mk II fighters into the NF.XVII with a Universal Nose able to house AI Mk VIII or the outstanding American AI Mk 10 (SCR-720). Newly built aircraft to this standard were called NF.XIX, with low-blown Merlin 25s and paddle-blade propellers. Last of the wartime 'Mozzies' was the NF.30, a Mk XIX with the high-blown two-stage Merlin 72, 76 or113. The Mk 30 was by far the most efficient Allied night-fighter of the war, and like earlier versions carried the war with cannon shells and special electronic-warfare devices into the heart of Germany.

New Technology

Though Britain pioneered the turbojet and actually got the Meteor I into squadron service ahead of any other jet in the world, few were ordered and it made little impact on the war. And the M.B.5, Spiteful, Vickers Type 432, Welkin and other new types never displaced the Spitfire and Mosquito.

The first Gloster G.40, built to specification E.28/39, is seen flying in 1943 with extra fins.

So ubiquitous was the Spitfire that the RAF hardly used any other British single-seat fighters in the later part of World War II, though there were plenty of new designs. The Spitfire itself was intended to be replaced by an extremely fast and agile machine, the Spiteful, which began life as a modified Spitfire fuselage riding on a totally new wing of only 210 sq ft (19.5 m) area and a laminar-flow section. With a wide-track landing gear and very powerful two-stage Griffon engine the Spiteful seemed ideal, and one of the variants, the F.16, was the UK's fastest piston-fighter at 494 mph (795 km/h): it would have been simple to assemble the airframe, engine and propeller differently to exceed 500 mph (805 km/h) by a substantial margin, but this good-looking machine never entered service. Not least of the unexpected results was that at high Mach numbers the new laminar wing was inferior to the old Spitfire wing, and almost certainly the post-war Attacker jet fighter would have been better had it had the old wing instead of the new one inherited from the Spiteful.

New Technology

The Martin-Baker M.B.5 was a superb aircraft in all respects, but happened to reach the service evaluation stage just as piston-engined fighters appeared obsolete. James Martin (later Sir James, pioneer of ejection seats) never did break into the closed-shop cartel of British fighter manufacturers.

The only other late-war fighters with a single piston engine were the Martin-Baker M.B.3 and M.B.5. The former was powered by a Sabre and carried the tremendous armament of six Hispano cannon, but was tragically destroyed in a fatal crash caused by engine failure on 12 September 1942. The M.B.5 was even better, and easily reached 460 mph (740 km/h) on its 2,340-hp (1746-kw) Griffon 83, driving a DH contra-rotating propeller, but despite outstanding engineering and good handling it was not put into production.

High-altitude requirement

Two technically interesting twin-engined fighters were built to specification F.7/41 calling for a high-altitude fighter with six cannon, a pressurised cockpit and two Merlin 61 engines. The

Though an outstanding fighter in most respects, the Supermarine Spiteful incorporated a completely new wing of so-called laminar-flow profile which at high subsonic Mach numbers proved markedly inferior to the old wing of the Spitfire! This particular Spiteful was the first of just 17 production aircraft which were given the mark number F.XIV.

Production Sea Hornet FR.20 fighter-reconnaisance aircraft serving with No. 801 Sqn from RNAS Ford in 1947. Later the Fleet Air Arm received the two-seat NF.21 night-fighter, which was appreciably slower.

Vickers Type 432 looked rather like a Mosquito but carried the fashionable Spitfire elliptical shapes to the limit, having elliptical wings, tailplane and fin/rudder unit. It flew in December 1942 and in many ways was an outstanding aircraft. Its rival, the Westland Welkin, flew a month earlier and was noted for its great span, adopted in order to reach the greatest possible altitude. In some respects the Welkin resembled a twin-Merlin development of the Whirlwind, but it was so much larger and heavier that performance was unimpressive, and the great span made rate of roll poor. There were many other shortcomings, and compressibility effects on the wing became evident at even shallow angles of dive, so that this sluggish machine could not catch other aircraft if they dived away. Despite this 67 production Welkins were delivered, and another was completed as a two-seater radar-equipped night-fighter.

A far better twin-engined fighter was the de Havilland Hornet. In many ways a smaller edition of

Most of the 67 production Westland Welkin F.I high-altitude interceptors were finished in overall PRU Blue, with Type B (red/blue) insignia. In some respects the greatest of all wartime ultra-high-flying fighters, the Welkin was crippled by poor rate of roll (and other snags) and never reached the RAF. A single aircraft in a later serial range (PF370) was completed as a two-seat radar-equipped night interceptor.

New Technology

Gloster Meteor

SPECIFICATION
Type: single-seat day fighter
Powerplant: (F.I.) two 1,700-lb
(771-kg) thrust Rolls-Royce
W.2B/23C Welland turbojets
Performance: maximum speed
415 mph (668 km/h) at 10,000 ft
(3050 m); service ceiling 40,000 ft
(12190 m)
Weights: empty 8,140 lb
(3692 kg); maximum take-off
13,795 lb (6257 kg)
Dimensions: span 43 ft 0 in
(13.11 m); length 41 ft 3 in
(12.57 m); height 13 ft 0 in
(3.96 m); wing area 374 sq ft
(34.74 m²)
Armament: four 20-mm
cannon

Gloster Meteor F.III of No.245 Sqn.

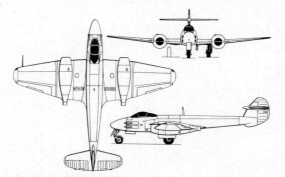

Gloster Meteor F.III

Gloster Meteor Mk I

Though not intended as a fighter, the Trent-Meteor is of historic importance as the world's first turboprop aircraft. It was built as a regular Meteor I fighter (EE227) and converted with Trent engines driving small five-blade propellers in September 1945.

the Mosquito, this could have been flown in 1941 instead of 1944, and would have been a most valuable combat aircraft with great range, performance and versatility. As it was, it just missed the war, though it later served as a single seat day interceptor and fighter-bomber with the RAF and FAA, and with the latter as a two-seat radar-equipped carrier-based night and all-weather fighter. The reason it did not fly in 1941 was that it was never ordered (and DH were overloaded with other work); when it did appear it was, like its predecessor, solely the result of initiative by the company.

One machine that could not have been a private venture by the company was the Gloster E.28/39, because this was built to fly the Whittle turbojet which, to the surprise of almost everyone except the tiny team at Power Jets, actually worked. The E.28/39 was a small and compact single-engined machine, sitting very low on tricycle landing gear and with the cockpit well

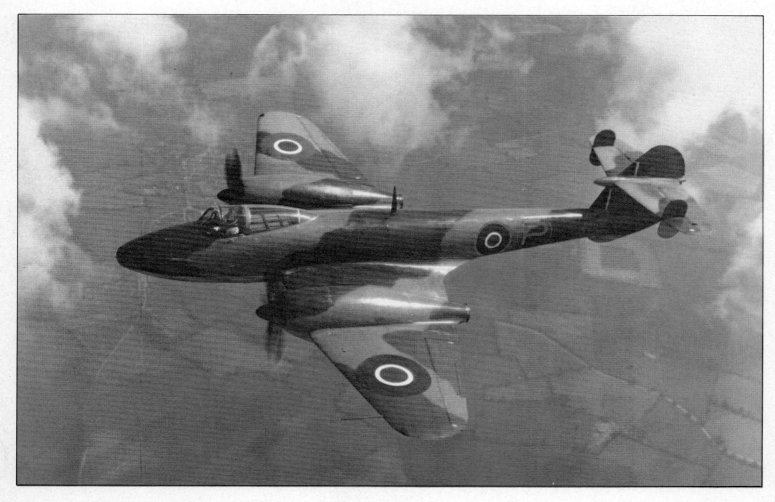

Taken in the last week of July 1944, this historic photograph shows the world's first regular squadron of jet fighters: No. 616 of the RAF (which still retained several Spitfires, seen in the background). Standing patrols against flying bombs were mounted from 27 July, two bombs being downed on 4 August. Note the fuel bowser (the first to have kerosene).

forward. Provision was made for four machine-guns firing ahead, but these were never fitted. Instead Gloster were assigned the more difficult task of building a fully operational jet fighter, to specification F.9/40. Two turbojets were to be used, and these were mounted well outboard on the sharply tapered wings, the cockpit being in the nose of the long slim fuselage with two (originally there were to be three) cannon on each side. The landing gear was a tricycle with levered suspension, and the tailplane was mounted very high on the fin.

The first F.9/40 flew on two DH H.1 engines (later named Goblin) on 5 March 1943. Other prototypes had the Power Jets W.2/500, Rover W.2B and Rolls-Royce W.2B/23, all variants of the Whittle W.2 design, and another had slim underslung nacelles for the Metrovick F.2 (later named Beryl). Development was quite rapid, the problems lying not with the engines but with such pedestrian things as the ailerons, rudder and nosewheel. Eventually the F.9/40 became the

Though the first prototype D.H.100 Vampire had graceful vertical tails of traditional de Havilland shape, the tops were cut off in the production F.I model which went into production at English Electric in 1944. In the author's view this was the best of all British wartime fighters, though it was a crude machine by American standards.

New Technology

Before going to join 2nd TAF in Belgium in January 1945 No. 616 Sqn was re-equipped with the Meteor III, with a much improved windscreen and sliding canopy. This photograph was taken in Germany in April 1945, by which time the Derwent-engined Mk III was in service.

Meteor F.I with the Rolls-Royce Welland, a derivative of the W.2B/23. They reached RAF No. 616 Sqn on 12 July 1944, the first operational jet fighter in the world. Almost at once they went into action against V-1 flying bombs, and as a temporary fault was found with the guns a few pilots downed bombs by tipping them over with a wing tip. From September 1944 Gloster delivered the improved Meteor F.III with many refinements including a sliding instead of hinged canopy; from the 16th example the Mk III had the Derwent I engine with 'straight through' combustion chambers, and late in the war longer engine nacelles were fitted.

Vampire just makes the war

Only one other British jet fighter was flown during the war. The de Havilland D.H.100, at first called Spider Crab but later named Vampire, was a smaller and most attractive machine with a layout that had been considered for the E.28/39. The engine was mounted in the rear of a short fuselage nacelle, fed by wing-root inlets, and the tail was carried on twin booms. Metal stressed-skin construction was used except for the nacelle, which was of wooden construction like the Mosquito. Armament comprised four cannon under the cockpit in the nose. The first Vampire flew on 20 September 1943 and demonstrated outstanding handling, but DH were overloaded and eventually production had to be assigned to English Electric, the first Mk I flying on 20 April 1945.

de Havilland Vampire

SPECIFICATION:
Type: single-seat day fighter
Powerplant: (F.I.) one de Havilland Goblin turbojet (first 41 aircraft DGn.1 of 2,700-lb (1225-kg) thrust
Performance: (full-rated engine) maximum speed 540 mph (869 km/h) at 20,000 ft (6095 m); service ceiling 44,000 ft (13410 m); range 730 miles (1175 km)
Weights: empty 6,372 lb (2890 kg); maximum take-off 8,578 lb (3891 kg)
Dimensions: span 40 ft 0 in (12.19 m); length 30 ft 9 in (9.37 m); height 8 ft 1 in (2.464 m); wing area 266 sq ft (24.7 m²)
Armament: four 20-mm Hispano cannon

Vampire F.I of No. 247 Sqn, Royal Air Force.

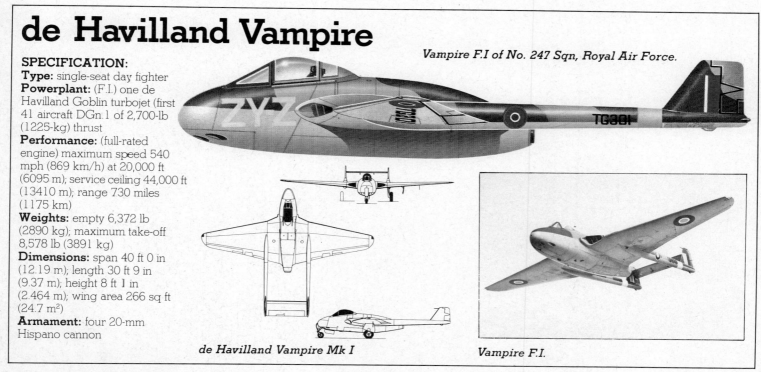

de Havilland Vampire Mk I

Vampire F.I.

Combat Aircraft Library

British
Fighters
of World War II

This superbly illustrated book graphically charts the development
of British fighters during the traumatic years of World War II.
Pitched unwillingly and ill-prepared into a war of survival
against the overwhelming strength and quality of Hitler's
Luftwaffe, British aircraft designers and airmen were
challenged to develop existing fighters and to produce new
types against a background of limited time, resources and
war-torn facilities.

But out of this unlikely scene came some of the finest
machines the world had ever seen: Spitfire, Hurricane,
Mosquito, Beaufighter, Typhoon and Tempest. Machines that
threw back the Luftwaffe from the skies of Britain and
eventually drove them from the air, land and seas of occupied
Europe.

These aircraft wrote the history of Britain in those war-ravaged
skies and were the greatest testament to the qualities of British
ingenuity, ability and will to survive.